Techniques of Becoming Wealthy

Techniques of Becoming Wealthy

by Richard H. Rush
and the Editors of U.S.News & World Report Books

Joseph Newman—Directing Editor

U.S.NEWS & WORLD REPORT BOOKS

A division of U.S.News & World Report, Inc.
WASHINGTON, D.C.

Contents

Illustrations

Tables and charts

Forms

Acknowledgments

Richard H. Rush and the Editors of *U.S. News & World Report Books* express their appreciation to the following:

The late J. Paul Getty, who, first as employer and later as friend of the author during more than two decades, inspired many of the activities described in this book.

Julie Rush, for her advice and optimism as business partner and wife of the author.

The personnel of the major auction houses, Christie's and Sotheby Parke Bernet, for their continuing assistance, particularly Clark, Nelson, Ltd., public relations firm of Sotheby Parke Bernet, and John Herbert, who performs a similar function for Christie's.

The late Dr. William Suida and his daughter and son-in-law, the Robert L. Mannings, for their advice on the purchase of art.

Fred R. Tansill of the Bird and Tansill law firm in Washington, D.C., for his guidance on the subject of minimizing taxes.

Attorney Harry Peden, Jr., of Greenwich, Connecticut, for advice regarding the use of trusts.

Editor Roslyn Grant of *U.S.News & World Report Books* for her assistance during the months of work on the manuscript for this book.

CHAPTER 1

The Will to Wealth

If asked, "Wouldn't you like to be wealthy?" many people would answer to the effect, "Yes, but wealth has never come my way." They believe that the person who has wealth either always had it or acquired it by some rare chance.

It is true that wealth is sometimes acquired by chance. Some people inherit it. Others, such as professional athletes or entertainers, have extraordinary talents that bring them riches. However, in most cases, wealth is accumulated not by chance but by a strong desire to become wealthy. We might say that wealth is directly proportional to the desire for wealth.

A constant "will to wealth" is necessary to accumulate wealth. If the qualities of perseverance and self-discipline to attain wealth are present, wealth is likely to follow. This "will to wealth" must be a firm resolve and a continuing one. In this respect it is like a resolve to stop smoking or to cut down on fattening foods. It may not be easy to develop this attitude but the longer it is maintained, the easier it becomes. Actually, it can be considerably easier than breaking the cigarette habit or losing weight.

One must combine this resolve with some of the major techniques for acquiring wealth. These techniques are something like the complete set of tools owned by a professional automobile mechanic. A great deal of work can be done on a car with a pair of pliers, a flat wrench, a screwdriver, and a hammer. You can even remove spark plugs with this combination. A complete set of tools, however, makes the job much easier and quicker, and almost certainly achieves a better result. This can also be said for the techniques of becoming wealthy. They are essentially tools or devices to enable the would-be wealth-builder to accomplish the job faster and better.

Many cases of wealth accumulation are the result of the employment of certain techniques by recipients of income, and it is these techniques that will be examined in this book, together with suitable examples of exactly how they are employed.

Income versus wealth

A widely held, erroneous belief is that a person who has a large income is wealthy. Although an income of some kind is required in order to accumulate a fund of wealth, large income is by no means synonymous with wealth.

A few years ago this writer was consulted by a Washington, D.C., management firm which had a very large computer manufacturing company as a client. The Washington office of this manufacturer had twelve executives. Their average annual salary was about $70,000.

The management firm was asked to conduct a survey of the twelve executives in order to make recommendations as to how they might be helped in the handling of

More Families Moving Into
Upper Income Brackets

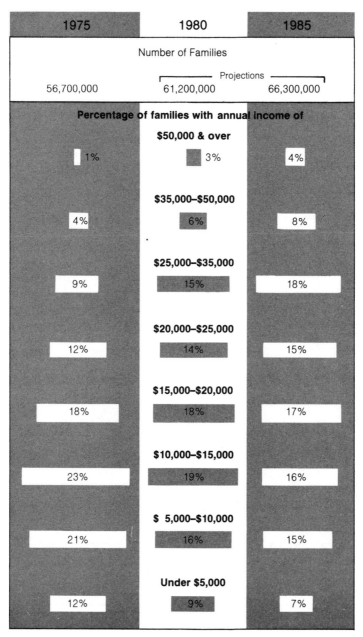

1975	1980	1985

Number of Families

┌──────── Projections ────────┐

| 56,700,000 | 61,200,000 | 66,300,000 |

Percentage of families with annual income of

$50,000 & over

| 1% | 3% | 4% |

$35,000–$50,000

| 4% | 6% | 8% |

$25,000–$35,000

| 9% | 15% | 18% |

$20,000–$25,000

| 12% | 14% | 15% |

$15,000–$20,000

| 18% | 18% | 17% |

$10,000–$15,000

| 23% | 19% | 16% |

$ 5,000–$10,000

| 21% | 16% | 15% |

Under $5,000

| 12% | 9% | 7% |

Source: The Conference Board

Number of Millionaires
Increasing Rapidly

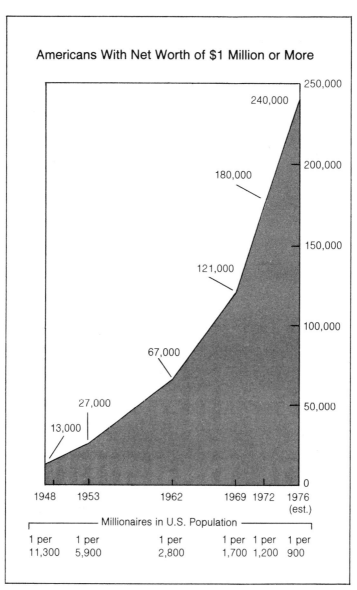

Americans With Net Worth of $1 Million or More

13,000 — 1948
27,000 — 1953
67,000 — 1962
121,000 — 1969
180,000 — 1972
240,000 — 1976 (est.)

Millionaires in U.S. Population

1948	1953	1962	1969	1972	1976
1 per 11,300	1 per 5,900	1 per 2,800	1 per 1,700	1 per 1,200	1 per 900

Source: U.S. Department of the Treasury

their personal finances. The survey revealed that not one of the twelve had much wealth. They had homes and they had insurance policies. Aside from these two usual assets, these executives had very little in cash, stocks, bonds, or other valuable holdings. They seemed to believe that their large incomes would continue forever and they therefore had no motivation to accumulate wealth.

Another characteristic was that their expenditures tended to increase as their incomes increased; they seemed compelled to spend what they received. A trip to the West Indies for a few days was no rarity, and in one case such a trip for the executive and his wife cost $4,500. A saving of $4,500 each year for twenty years at 8 percent compound interest will produce a capital fund of over $200,000.

Not only is income no measure of the accumulation of wealth, it sometimes seems that the larger the income, the smaller the savings—certainly the smaller as a percentage of income. This impression is reinforced by a review of the size of the estates left by high earners, such as prominent lawyers, surgeons, and business executives.

The price tag on "wealth"

When we think of accumulating wealth, we might ask, "What constitutes wealth?" The answer may vary from person to person. The late multibillionaire J. Paul Getty, for example, would not listen to criticism of his business policies from anyone who had not made $1 million. He believed that a person who had not been able to accumulate that sum was not qualified to criticize him.

Capital amounting to $1 million certainly qualifies a person to be considered wealthy, even in this era of inflation. We might, however, lower the definition of "wealth" to a quarter of a million dollars and even to $200,000. On capital of $200,000 one can easily obtain a fairly secure life-long return of $20,000 a year. It is not extremely difficult over the years to increase this return to, say, $25,000 a year—in good times and in bad, in times of high interest rates and in times of low interest rates.

Saving and investing

If your present annual income is between $15,000 and $25,000 and you are finding it difficult to manage on your earnings, you may feel that you could never accumulate capital of $200,000. But others have done it. Among them is a former government employee in Washington, D.C., whose maximum annual salary in all of his working life was $11,000 and whose average salary was far lower than this maximum. This man decided that he would like to have a substantial amount of wealth, but he did not seem to have any special field of business interest that might enable him to accumulate it—or even to develop much of an income. He married late in life and his wife earned a moderate salary. The only method he could employ as a means of developing wealth was saving money, and save he did, with the result that he was able to retire in his middle fifties with over $200,000 in capital and with an annual income of over $20,000.

Saving money by controlling expenditures is a major technique of becoming wealthy. How it is done will be fully explained later in this book. Another major technique is buying a home as an investment. This technique too will be outlined in detail, and you will learn how a couple who began twenty years ago with a down payment of $5,500 on a house costing $17,500 "moved up" to their present house valued at $340,000 although they have invested only the equivalent of $148 a month in the two decades during which they have been investing in homes.

Renting out one's home is another important technique for the accumulation of capital, since this procedure provides the homeowner with a fixed-dollar return as well as an equity investment. Depreciation of the property is the method by which renting one's home can seem to be a losing proposition although it is quite the opposite, since it protects income against taxation. As one example of the use of this technique you will read later of a couple who received a 70 percent annual return on the cash they had invested in their home by renting it.

Not only a home but also its furnishings can contribute to wealth. Paintings and drawings, antique furniture, clocks, silverware, glassware, and porcelain are among the collectibles that are in a long-term uptrend. Even the cars in your garage can be excellent investments if chosen wisely. So can the wine in your cellar. If you will take the time to acquire sufficient knowledge of a particular collectible you will find, as others have, that great buys can be made with very small sums of money.

A prime example of this is a man who had been a director of a small museum in New York City where his maximum salary was about $12,000 a year. The museum closed in 1975 and he was out of a job. He has been out of a job ever since. But he does not need one. Over the years he had bought old master paintings, mainly of the Italian school, for sums usually ranging from $500 to about $50 each. He also had bought old master drawings for sums that did not range far upward from $10 apiece. He had paid for these paintings and drawings out of his salary. Now he has about 500 paintings and 1,000 drawings. A short time ago his family decided that they needed a newer, finer house than the one they had bought for $26,000 in the 1950s. The new house they chose cost $210,000. In order to buy it the collector of old masters sold just five of his paintings. This man supports himself and his family by selling a painting or two each year for $25,000 or $50,000 or whatever sum he needs. When he sells a painting he does not pay the ordinary income tax on the profit but only the capital gains tax, which is about one-half of the full rate.

Later in this book you will read about many other instances in which enormous profits have been made by those who have invested in the rapidly rising market for collectibles. And you will be given guidance for employing this technique for acquiring wealth.

Other major techniques

Another challenging, and certainly major, technique for becoming wealthy is to start a business of your own and operate it until it can be sold for a large profit. While this may sound like a highly difficult feat, it has been accomplished by many wealth-builders. As just one example here, with others to follow in a later chapter, consider the case of a man who at the age of thirty-nine found himself out of a job. Try as he might, he could not find employment even remotely like the jobs he had held, nor at anything like his former salaries in government and in business. So he decided to try his hand as an insurance agent, specializing in mobile homes. He became the "leg man" in the field and his wife-to-be became the "office staff." In the first full year of business the two-person firm had an income in six figures, and the prospects for the future were bright. At this point they decided to accept an offer for the business. The couple received over $200,000 for the business they had developed and operated for less than three years. Then they went into another enterprise with their new fund of capital.

Whatever method is chosen to acquire a nest egg, a very material part of the wealth-building process is to make the accumulated assets earn. This technique will be explained with regard to depositing money in banks, making loans, and investing in securities and mortgages in order to receive a return of at least 12 percent per annum on one's money.

The use of trusts is an important technique which is little understood by many people who would like to build wealth. A detailed discussion of how trusts can be employed by even those at the relatively lower levels of income and wealth is therefore included.

The Nation's Wealth
And Its Owners

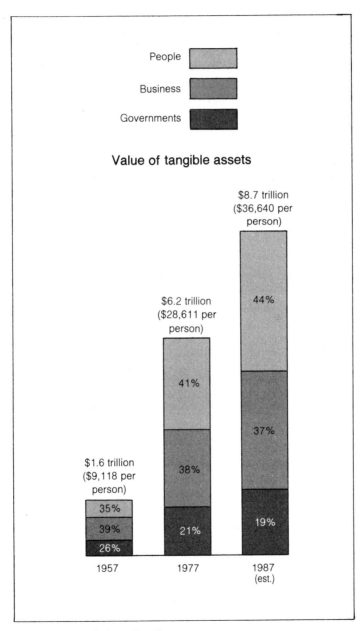

People

Business

Governments

Value of tangible assets

$8.7 trillion
($36,640 per
person)

$6.2 trillion
($28,611 per
person)

$1.6 trillion
($9,118 per
person)

44%

41%

38%

35%

39%

37%

26%

21%

19%

1957

1977

1987
(est.)

Source: Based on The Conference Board figures

It is essential that the wealth-builder forecast income and taxes annually. Further on in this book you will learn why this technique is essential and how you can use it to increase your capital. This explanation will include the use of "tax shields" to protect your income. These shields do not in any way result in tax evasion, which is illegal. They can, however, result in tax avoidance, which is taking advantage of provisions in the law so that your tax bill is less than it otherwise would be.

And, finally, this book will tell you why more people are not wealthy despite the fact that so many methods for acquiring wealth are available to them. It will also tell you what can be done by those who wish to overcome the negative personal characteristics that have prevented them from joining the thousands of wealth-builders in this country.

With an annual income of at least $15,000 and with a will to become wealthy, the techniques described in the following chapters should help you toward your goal.

CHAPTER 2

Characteristics of the Wealth-Builders

Although it may seem that anyone who puts his mind to it and persists can become wealthy, successful wealth-builders have certain motivations and personal characteristics that pushed them in the direction of becoming wealthy. These driving forces remain with them for the rest of their lives. Often the characteristics and the turn of mind that can be called a "will to wealth" are developed over a period of years, and sometimes fairly late in life.

Why do some people accumulate a fund of wealth? Why don't they just spend as the money comes in? No one lives forever, so why do they worry about building a nest egg? What are the motives of wealth-builders?

Motive number one: to be independent

The desire to be independent of corporate or organizational discipline is the most important motive of wealth-builders. Many of them do not fit in and do not want to fit into any organization, business or otherwise.

Working in an organization is not an especially easy means of obtaining an income. It often requires a good many personality adjustments. The individual must be subordinated to the entire group working together. The position of the employee is very much like the position of the private in the army, particularly if the employee is not very far up the organizational ladder. The organization moves as a unit, and the individual is only a very small cog in the machine. The employee's job is rigidly circumscribed and the duties must be performed in a prescribed way.

The independent spirit frets under these conditions. Very often such an employee feels unable to "grow." Often the very able person, the hard worker, feels superior to coworkers, and even to the boss. Why should such a person have to fit in, work like the other employees, and be unable to rise above them? An individual of this type resents having to clear everything with the boss, particularly if the employee works harder than the boss and feels at least as competent as the boss.

This antiorganizational feeling leads to the next step—the desire to be one's own boss. Very often the employee is right in believing that the corporation is not set up to recognize individual effort or to reward the outstanding person who is willing to work on company problems evenings and weekends. Nor does the corporation seem willing to promote the standout employee over others who have seniority. Also, outstanding work done within the organization may antagonize colleagues and even the boss, who may think the subordinate has an eye on his or her job.

The person who has the characteristics required to build wealth may want more recognition than the organization can or will give, and may want it right now. Such an employee prefers not to wait for years until someone higher up in the organization retires, making it possible for the employee to move up a rung on the ladder.

The potential wealth-builder is often willing to work harder than is possible within the organization on a nine-to-five, five-days-a-week basis.

It is not a great jump in the thinking of such an employee to realize that working successfully for the organization means it would be possible to work successfully for oneself.

The advantage of working for oneself is that all work, no matter how long or how hard, will redound to the benefit of the individual, not to any impersonal organization.

In the business world of today, the one who takes the route of private enterprise and wealth-building is the great exception. University and graduate school education in the field of business administration is directed toward making a young person ready to occupy a position in a department of a company, at best as head of a department—production, finance, sales, statistics, accounting.

The longer the young person remains on the corporate payroll, the harder it is to opt for private enterprise. The employee has too much to lose in the way of a reliable paycheck and fringe benefits, including a pension.

Sometimes the choice of working for a company or becoming one's own boss is not up to the employee. An employee may lose a job and decide to try self-employment, which then results in the new entrepreneur becoming oriented toward profit and capital, in a word, wealth. Once this route is taken, the person may well not return to any corporate payroll.

Motive number two: to compete

For most wealth-builders, the accumulation of wealth is more of a game than a passion for acquiring more money than one knows what to do with. To the true wealth-builder the activity of building wealth is like tennis, golf, or bridge to other individuals. The wealth-builder likes to excel at the "game" in competition with others; and in poor times is usually willing to admit to not having done so well, but often adds that the result was considerably better than that of some friends and colleagues.

In entrepreneur or wealth-building circles stories are often told of successful financial ventures. It is, however, rare for wealth-builders to reveal how much money they have or to boast of having more money than someone else. The objective is to win a game, not to be the wealthiest. One wealth-builder is proud of the fact that 1973 was his biggest year in eighteen years, and 1974 and 1975 were close behind. How much he made is more or less immaterial. What is important to him is that he bucked the depression trend and, to a considerable extent, outfoxed the economic statistics.

To the wealth-builder, percentages are important. Such a person becomes upset when realizing a yearly appreciation of, say, only 10 percent while a friend realizes 15 percent. That the friend has perhaps $10 million while the wealth-builder has only a few hundred thousand dollars is unimportant. That the friend's performance is better is very important. The upsetting thing is not winning the game.

Motive number three: to be secure

There is little question that wealth provides personal security and eases life's financial shocks.

A suitable financial security objective might be to have enough cash and other liquid assets to provide for a period of two or three years without any income.

When one who has wealth returns home at night on the commuter train some peace of mind is gained by knowing that the wealth will see the family through a recession while others on the train, many of them enjoying fine incomes, have little stored away for a rainy day.

The "depression philosophy" is, of course, basic to the thinking of a good many business people today. If during the Great Depression one lived in a house without central heating, electricity, telephone, or indoor plumbing, and without money to pay taxes and make mortgage payments, the motive is very strong to get as far away from that life as possible—and the feeling is not likely to disappear, no matter how much time passes since those unhappy depression years.

It becomes clear to anyone who has experienced the financial vicissitudes of business, including the recessions of 1948, 1953, 1957, 1961, 1970, and 1974, that financial security is highly desirable.

Another aspect of this motive is establishing security for one's old age. A truly outstanding salesman, as one example, was always trying to build up a fund of capital to "provide for my old age." He retired at fifty-two because he felt he had enough funds and independent income for the rest of his days. After about six months in retirement, he came back to the business world in order, so he said, "to provide more for my old age." He had also become bored with retirement. He took a selling job on the basis of pure commissions. Within one year his commissions were running at an annual rate of $100,000. Such performance is to an extent standard procedure for wealth-builders, although the degree of this man's success in so short a time is unusual.

Some might think that financial security should be placed first among the motives that drive people to become wealthy, but it does not really seem to occupy that position in the minds of most wealth-builders. Perhaps those who go directly after financial security do not have the most effective motive for accumulating wealth.

Motive number four: to live luxuriously

Wealth as the "badge of success" belongs about here in the listing of motives for the accumulation of riches.

It should be remembered that over the centuries, wealth has to a great extent been synonymous with social class. Money has been the means of rising socially and of securing positions of distinction—in the clergy, the army, the foreign service, the government, and even the nobility. This is probably an underlying factor in spurring some people on to acquire wealth.

Wealth can buy things that advertise one's success in life, such as a Rolls-Royce car or a country club membership. However, not many people say, in effect, "I want wealth because then I can advertise my success and improve my social standing." More often it is after securing wealth that people think in terms of owning a Rolls-Royce or joining a country club. The acquisition of luxuries does not seem to be a major motive for wealth-builders.

The new group of wealth-builders

A number of years ago this writer attended a conference in Miami Beach, Florida. It was the first time he had been in Miami Beach, or in Florida, for that matter. One thing impressed him above everything else that he saw in Miami—the obvious display of wealth. He recalls counting the number of Cadillacs that passed him in the space of one minute. He wondered who owned them and how the owners secured their money. Then he tried to estimate the number of Cadillacs in all of Miami at that time, and came up with a guess of 1,000.

At this point he decided to find out the sources of wealth of these and other Cadillac owners—what businesses they were in, how long they had taken to arrive at their present state of wealth, what techniques they used to accumulate their wealth. This survey broadened from Miami, and eventually included places all the way from Los Angeles to Port Chester, New York.

Over the years the questions were answered. The survey also revealed that almost all of these owners of wealth were business entrepreneurs rather than employees of corporations.

While generalization is probably inaccurate as regards any particular individual, and any individual is made up of many motives and characteristics, still it is possible to list the attributes or characteristics of this group of wealth-builders:

1. *Their wealth is of recent origin.* Obviously the wealth of the Rockefellers, Mellons, Fords, et al., is not of recent date, and we are not referring to this group of industrial leaders when we list the characteristics of wealth-builders. The senior group may contain just as many wealthy people as the new group (in numbers, of course, not in the size of individual holdings), but the old group is distinctly different. The business methods of the older group are different. More important, the enterprises operated by the senior group are much larger than those operated by the "new group" and, in general, of a different nature. This difference will become clear as we discuss the other characteristics of this new group of the wealthy.

A very large percentage of the new group of wealth-builders has secured wealth since World War II, and many have done so during the last decade or two. Even though many of them were in business during and before the war, their major accumulations of wealth have been since the war, some accumulations having been accomplished quite recently. Most members of the group began with absolutely no inherited wealth. Many have literally risen from rags to riches.

2. *They are extremely astute.* Everyone in the new group seems to have an acute "nose for business." There is nothing academic in their makeup, and they are certainly not typical corporation executives with an organizational viewpoint.

3. *They are extremely competitive.* They compete in

Who Our Millionaires Are

Marital Status

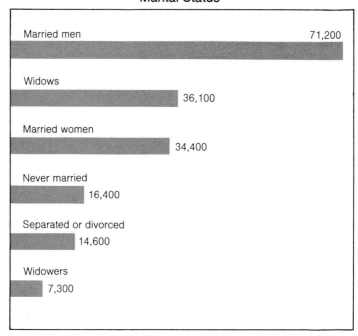

Married men — 71,200

Widows — 36,100

Married women — 34,400

Never married — 16,400

Separated or divorced — 14,600

Widowers — 7,300

Age

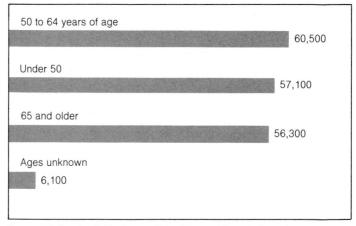

50 to 64 years of age — 60,500

Under 50 — 57,100

65 and older — 56,300

Ages unknown — 6,100

Sources: U.S. Department of the Treasury, National Bureau of Economic Research

the price at which they offer their product or service, the terms they offer, and the additional services they are willing to supply.

They are by no means philosophical in the face of declining sales or poor profit showings. They meet any and all competition by reducing prices, making special deals, or taking other steps to beat their rivals.

They do not hesitate to cut prices drastically to sell a slow-moving item or to clear out a losing line of goods. They promptly forget about their losses and move on to something else.

4. *They have an ability to "see a deal."* They seem to have an eye for economic opportunity. They also have the ability to act on what they see without delay.

Several years ago a lawyer-entrepreneur in Washington offered some gratuitous advice which turned out to be invaluable to this writer. He said, "Stop looking for retainers and fees and start looking for 'deals.' "

This writer looked at him blankly and asked, "What's a deal?"

He answered the question by taking from a pile of papers lying on his desk a check payable to him in the amount of $25,000.

"This represents a deal," he said. "I was given $25,000 to undertake to get a certain foreign government to permit an American company to drill for oil in its country. I was to receive another $25,000 if I was successful in securing this permission. I was successful, and this is the second check for $25,000. But much more important, I have been given 5 percent of the stock of the new drilling company. Of course, the whole thing is a gamble. Maybe the drilling operation will produce no oil; but it is reasonable to assume from a geologic survey that it will. I confidently expect that my 5 percent of the stock will be worth several million dollars in the future. In any event, I have $50,000 in cash plus this possibility. That's a deal."

Any important financier, investment banking house, or

bank has hundreds of "deals" presented in the course of a year. The trick is to determine which few are the good ones and then reject the rest. Probably 90 per cent or more of all business propositions involving new ventures are unsound or otherwise unworkable. The new wealth-builders seem to have an almost uncanny sense to sift out this under-10-percent group of potential successes and make sound financial and organizational plans to realize their potential.

5. *They are willing to give something in order to get something.* For the most part, they are not hoggish. This writer recalls having sat in with a major wealth-builder listening to a potential deal involving a proposed mortgage on a property located on Long Island, New York. At the conclusion of the presentation to the "money man," he asked the applicants a number of questions. After receiving the answers he asked them, "Would you gentlemen be satisfied with 50 percent of the profit?" The immediate reply was, "Yes." At this point the money man committed himself to a sum in six figures.

After the general terms of the new investment had been agreed upon and the applicants for the money had left, this writer asked the financier, "Why were you so liberal regarding the profit when you supply all the capital, and how were you able to give this proposition an O.K. so quickly?"

He replied, "You have to give in order to get them to produce the business and as far as the details of their proposition go, I know that type of business. What they said made sense to me."

As another example, years ago the president of a large insurance company asked this writer whether he was personally acquainted with the president of a certain American airline. The reply was that he knew the man well. The insurance company president then said that he owned a Mexican airline which wanted permission to fly to the United States from Mexico. He said he had secured permission from the Mexican government to enter into an agreement with an American airline whereby there would be an interchange of equipment between both airlines for service between Mexican cities and American cities. The insurance company president felt that if he could make such an arrangement, the American airline would stand a good chance of securing permission from the U.S. Civil Aeronautics Board to conduct such an operation, and the American airline could make large overwater planes available to the Mexican airline, which did not own such planes.

This writer's mission was only to get the president of the American airline to agree to the proposition; it was not to get the Civil Aeronautics Board to agree or to see that the final agreement resulted in actual joint flights. For simply getting this agreement from the president of the American airline $1,500 a month would be paid to this writer for at least a year.

It took just one visit to secure the agreement of the president of the American airline. The fee had been earned. The insurance company president was willing to pay $1,500 a month for a year for something he obviously valued highly, no matter how much or how little work it took to accomplish the result.

6. *They are willing to work and to sacrifice to arrive at their goal.* This is one "rule" adhered to by virtually every member of the new wealth-builders.

In the early days of their business activities, working seven days a week and sixteen hours a day is not at all uncommon. In fact, the "early days" might continue for years.

It is a maxim of wealth-building that the greater the effort and the more time spent, the greater the chance of success. A nine-to-five day five days a week will almost always be insufficient. Anyone trying to build wealth will find that wealth has to be worked for.

7. *They literally "go for broke."* The new wealth-

builders make an almost superhuman effort to succeed. This effort is continued for long periods of time if need be. Very often they borrow every cent they can lay their hands on for the business and plow back every cent of earnings until they are sure they have achieved success. Until they have succeeded in the enterprise they generally do not diversify their investments. That comes much later.

8. *A relatively large proportion are not highly educated in business administration.* For that matter, a very large proportion are not educated in anything, and many have only a secondary school education. There is no question that a knowledge of the techniques of operating a business enterprise would be of benefit to them, as would a Master of Business Administration degree from the Harvard Business School or some other prestigious school. However, although many, if not most, of the wealthbuilders lack such formal education, they are able to succeed without it.

Two things might be said against formal education in business administration as regards success in building business and in building wealth: (1) Such formal education tends to place too much stress on departmental problems and not enough emphasis on top-level problems and particularly on how to find a business need and fill it, and (2) formal education tends to place business thinking in a straitjacket, eliminating flexibility of mind and the ability to synthesize all of the business factors rapidly in order to arrive at a decision and a course of action.

9. *The majority of them are young.* By young, we mean under fifty years of age, and many of them are considerably younger than fifty.

A number of them began building wealth in their thirties, and in ten years achieved a good deal toward accomplishing their business and financial goals.

There are, of course, great exceptions to the rule of building wealth while one is young. The late Arthur Vining Davis, who was board chairman of the Aluminum Company of America, carried out a major part of his wealth-building activities in Florida land when he was in his nineties.

J. Paul Getty, who had perhaps as much as $3 billion when he died at the age of eighty-three, was generally unknown when he was in his sixties. Between the 1950s and the 1970s his wealth was multiplied about ten times. When this writer represented him in Washington, D.C., in 1952, Getty's name was almost unknown and one had to make a point of building him up and indicating that "J. Paul Getty is a really significant businessman."

10. *They usually do not have corporate backgrounds.* For the most part, they have not been employed as corporation executives. The corporate experience of many of them was, if it existed at all, at a very low level. Those with corporate backgrounds appear to have worked for large corporations only long enough to find out that they could do much better on their own.

11. *Their business decisions are bold.* They arrive at a decision quickly, act quickly, and follow up quickly to see that the decision is implemented.

12. *A relatively small portion of the group might be characterized as "pirates."* If, for instance, they see a business enterprise that it would be advantageous for them to control, they act rapidly and systematically to secure control of it. If they secure control, they often set about operating the company as if it were theirs, as if all of the funds of the company, regardless of other stockholders, belong to them to do with as they wish. The new wealth-builders are often backed up fully by trusted, yet sometimes unscrupulous, lawyers who pull out every stop to maintain control for their clients and help them avoid legal troubles. They may raise defenses against the obligation of their clients to pay debts or to live up to agreements. They may, on technicalities, try to revoke guarantees that their clients have given.

13. *Almost all of them operate a one-person show.* A recent advertisement in a magazine was placed by an electrical products company looking for new high-level researchers. The ad read, in substance, "A brilliant stand-out? No! One of a team that works together to produce a result." There was a picture of an apparently congenial group of men working on a project together.

The new group of wealth-builders does not fit this pattern at all. While they may want advice from others, they are the supreme commanders in their respective organizations. It is they who make not only the major decisions but also many of the minor ones.

When this writer first went to work in business—in an oil company—the true head of the company seemed to be the operating committee. The operating committee wanted such-and-such information, and the operating committee decided this and that. Although the company had a president, he seemed to sit on the operating committee as its impartial chairman.

Not so with the new wealth-building entrepreneurs. Each of them is the operating committee. They are not one of a group of nice people working toward decisions and results arrived at by cooperative effort.

14. *They are extremely flexible.* They face reality and take action to suit the times and the business situation. An example of a finance company illustrates this characteristic of the new wealth-builders. For several years the principal business of the finance company was mobile homes—conditional sales contracts and chattel mortgages which the mobile home buyer paid off in monthly installments. The president of the company saw delinquencies increasing at a rapid rate. His decision was quickly made—out of mobile home finance immediately and into another type of finance. But the main line chosen by the company's president to replace mobile homes was pre-fabricated homes. It soon became clear that this area was filled with "no-pay problems" too, so he got out of this

business and into conventional real estate mortgages, on which the company concentrated for many years with great financial success.

This immediate response to business problems has its weaknesses too. The new wealth-builders do not seem to see the long-term implications of business decisions. They do not appear willing to weather a storm if the rainbow seems far off.

They do not try very hard to anticipate how economic events or competition will affect them over a period of, say, five years. Their attitude is: Five years is a long time. Why worry about what is going to happen in five years if profits are good right now, and why try to stick it out if business is poor right now? They will cross the bridge when they come to it.

One such example of shortsightedness was the mobile home business when it first boomed. Every dealer seemed to be making money in the then new industry. No matter how inexperienced they were or how little capital they had, they could get credit to launch themselves as mobile home dealers.

But on every sale the dealer was "recourse." If the retail buyer did not make his payments, the bank financing the sale required the dealer to pay off. One dealer who had about $100,000 of net worth was recourse on sales contracts worth about $2 million. If one-fourth of this "paper" defaulted, the dealer would have to pay $500,000 to the bank. Even if he could raise the $500,000, a loss of just 20 percent on the resale of the $500,000 worth of mobile homes, or $100,000, would wipe out his entire net worth. This is exactly what happened to a large number of dealers. They might well have seen the handwriting on the wall when their business volume was at its peak and sold out at that time. Few of them did.

Another example of failure to see ahead occurred in the specialized mortgage business throughout the United

States in the period 1973 to 1975, particularly in the New York area. Specialized mortgages—large first mortgages and second mortgages—always paid off well. There were some foreclosures, of course, but when a property was sold at a foreclosure sale, there was generally enough realized to pay off both the first mortgage holder and the second mortgage holder.

Then fuel bills mounted in response to the Organization of Petroleum Exporting Countries' quadrupling of the price of crude petroleum. Electric bills rose in response too. The wage demands of maintenance workers increased greatly. Taxes rose in response to bigger municipal deficits. Rent increases could not cover the increased costs, particularly with record high rates on mortgages.

Defaults and foreclosure sales increased. The real estate market became glutted with forced sales. There were fewer and fewer buyers at foreclosure sales. Prices realized at the sales went down. Not enough was realized to cover the second mortgages and even the first in many cases. An apartment house in the best part of New York City's Park Avenue defaulted. Back taxes and back first mortgage payments for this building amounted to $400,000, including a small first mortgage. There was a second mortgage of $1,900,000. The second mortgage holders "wrote off" their entire investment of $1,900,000. The apartment house could have been acquired for $400,000.

The lack of foresight resulted in real estate becoming the industry with probably the most business failures in the entire period from 1945 to 1975.

15. *They specialize in industries that do not require a great deal of fixed assets.* They do not like to have their capital tied up in unsalable assets. They would not like to put a major proportion of their funds into an aluminum rolling mill, let us say. They would rather have the funds in notes receivable of less than a year's duration. They

also like to have assets that can be borrowed against at a bank, or on which they can sell stock to the public, assets which require as little of their own capital as possible. Some of the business opportunities in which they like to place their funds are:

• Real estate, including syndications, shopping centers, recreation centers, land developments—although many of the entrepreneurs went through the "wringer" on some of these enterprises during the recent recession.

• Finance companies.

• Wholesale and retail outlets and chains of supermarkets and discount houses. They like cut-rate businesses because cut-rate means competitive advantage.

• Brokerage organizations, whether of stock, investments, business, insurance, or real estate. Big business can often be done, resulting in big total commissions, with little or no employment of their own capital.

• Insurance businesses, particularly insurance wholesalers and organizations that reinsure with underwriters, as well as credit life, health, and accident insurance businesses.

• Service companies, and sometimes combination service and asset companies, such as the new burglar alarm and burglar telephone exchanges. Little outlay is required and business is burgeoning. The total markup is high and new customers are easy to develop in the present "scare era."

16. *They go into high-yield businesses.* One of the new wealth-builders/entrepreneurs was asked what he realized as an annual return on his capital. After some figuring, he replied, "About 24 percent a year."

The new group may go into low-markup businesses such as supermarkets, appliance wholesaling, and cut-rate retailing, but these businesses often provide a healthy return on invested capital.

The high return is achieved by such policies as charging very high rates on the funds they lend others, going after volume sales, securing leverage through borrowing, and financing with the public through the issuance of stock or other participations.

17. *They seek businesses with distinct tax advantages.* They like real estate ownership because it allows not only depreciation but accelerated depreciation for tax purposes. Such depreciation often provides a red figure on the asset or business and this red figure is applied to their other income so that they realize relatively large tax-protected incomes. They are also in businesses that allow the establishment of relatively large reserves for bad debts. Such reserves also provide tax savings. They protect their income against taxes in many other ways, which will be gone into more fully later in this book.

18. *Their business emphasis is significantly different.* They do not promote their products or their services as being the best available. They do not strive to offer the highest quality. Instead, they have their eyes strictly on financial results.

One might well ask, "Don't all business people have their eyes primarily on profits?"

The answer is, "Yes, they do, but the new wealth-builders have their eyes more on the financial returns than on the superiority of the products or services they offer."

There are still business managements that want to produce only the best and will not change their thinking even though they may suffer financially. Automobile-maker Enzo Ferrari is one of these and has always been. Mercedes-Benz may be another. Ferrari would not change his thinking or his objectives even though at one time he had to announce that it was necessary for him to close his automobile production plant.

If the new wealth-builders found themselves in a situation in which little or no profit could be expected from offering the best product or service of its type, a large number of them would make one of two choices: (1) offer a less expensive product or service in order to reach a larger number of buyers, or (2) sell out or otherwise liquidate the business.

As a rule, the new wealth-builders are far less idealistic than the old ones, although when we look back to the early years of this century, we find robber barons and oil monopolists, among other nonidealistic businessmen of that time.

To summarize, the new wealth-builders involve themselves in businesses and investments in which they can employ as many of the wealth-building techniques as possible.

3

Controlling Your Expenditures

As income increases so do expenditures. This is a principle afflicting almost everyone. No matter how high income goes, expenditures tend to creep up to its level so that nothing or very little is saved.

We need only recall the dozen executives of a large corporation who were discussed in Chapter 1. Their average annual income was about $70,000. Although some had an equity in their homes and insurance policies, they owned very little else. One wonders how, in the early 1970s, they could receive a gross income of $5,830 a month, or almost $1,500 every week, and still put nothing away. The answer, of course, is that they developed ways of squandering their income, such as a weekend in the Bahamas at a cost of $4,500.

Many high-income earners develop what might be

called "the philosophy of spending." The director of sci-
entific research of a large corporation makes an annual
salary well into six figures. Previously he was a government official in Washington, earning a far lower salary.
Expressing his attitude toward the possibility of accumulating wealth, he said: "I couldn't possibly save anything.
I don't have enough left over after taxes and the expenses
of living, and even if I should be able to accumulate any
savings, what am I offered as an outlet for my money?
Bad investments! What I need is not a 50 percent tax on
my salary but a 35 percent tax. An economist has demonstrated that if the 'tax loopholes' were eliminated, then all
I would have to pay is 35 percent tax. That's what I need.
Nothing else."

This philosophy of "can't save" runs throughout the
population—from top business executives to taxi drivers.

The resolve to save

The whole philosophy of "whatever I do I can't save" is
a passive, negative one. The resolve to control expenditures and to save money is a very major one. After one
has followed the resolve to save for a time, saving becomes much easier—unlike a resolve to give up smoking
or to diet. In other words, pressure does not build up to
stop saving and the body most certainly does not suffer.

The choice is just this: to spend as the money comes in,
or to build a fund of capital which will make one able in
the future to purchase important items that one otherwise could not afford or to become financially independent of a job (for at least long enough to find another
source of income) or to provide for a comfortable living
when one retires. These are three benefits of establishing
a fund of wealth. Another might be to establish one's own
business, either before or after retirement. Some organizations offer such early retirement that one might very
well undertake a new business after retiring.

The resolve to control expenditures and save money is

Personal Debt Increases
As Income Rises

Although total personal income in the United States was 10 percent higher at the end of 1976 than at the end of 1975, personal debt also increased 10 percent in the same period. The end-1976 total of $178.8 billion in consumer installment debt included $60.5 billion in automobile credit, $11.5 billion in mobile home credit, $8.8 billion in home-improvement credit, $14.1 billion in revolving credit, and $83.9 billion for all other consumer goods plus personal loans. The chart shows the extent that consumers are in debt to various types of creditors.

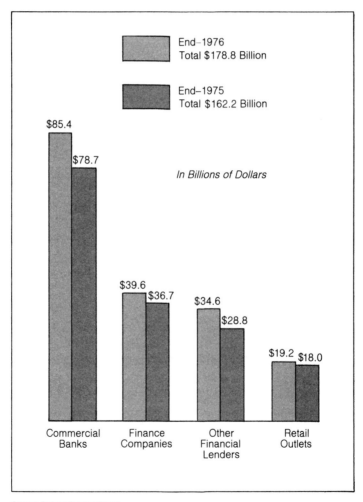

Source: Federal Reserve Board

central to wealth-building. If the individual can make this resolve, about 25 percent of the battle is won and 25 percent of the savings goal has in effect been reached.

How and why expenditures increase

These are the most usual reasons that expenditures keep pace with income:

1. In the first place, a person with a job and a good income in a sense lives in a "never-never land" in which the employee's income will be secure regardless of what takes place in the employing company or in the economy. Then when layoffs come and the company or the country goes through a period of hard times the employee's belief in a secure income is shattered.

Everyone receiving a salary or wages should consider the very real possibility of being laid off or dropped at any time in the future, whether the possibility is great or minimal. By seeing such a possibility as being real the employee is inclined to control expenditures and save.

2. Thorstein Veblen's theory of "conspicuous consumption and emulation" is certainly as valid today as when it was first expounded. A young couple bought a very satisfactory home in the prestigious New York suburb of New Canaan, Connecticut. There they developed friends in the community. Most of the husbands were commuters to business in New York City. One thing that the young couple noted time after time was "the goal of the $150,000 house." Everyone seemed to be enchanted with the idea of owning a house that cost $150,000, not simply because at the time $150,000 would buy a very fine house in New Canaan but also because one could then tell friends, "My house cost $150,000."

3. Another result of this same driving force is the calculation of income against outgo with the objective of demonstrating that "if we are careful about our other cash outlays, then we can afford" the fine new house, or

the second home, or the new Cadillac, or whatever is wanted.

This rationalization of buying something that obligates a great deal of one's income works like this: "Our present mortgage payments are $500 a month. If we buy the new house the mortgage payments will amount to $700 a month. If, however, we cut our entertainment expenses, including liquor, by $200 a month, we will be able to afford the new house."

It sounds easy at the time, as most rationalizations do, but more often than not the new house eliminates all possibility of saving (other than the amortization included in the $700 monthly payments) and may even result in spending more than is earned, thus reducing whatever fund of savings the family has.

4. Impulse buying is often a tremendous thief of income. When an individual goes into a store he or she generally buys something, and the more time spent in stores the more buying done, with consequent inroads on income. If, however, one avoids visiting the shops with all of their tempting merchandise, the impulse-buying problem is solved. What one does not see, one has no impulse to buy. One can either browse in stores on a Saturday, let us say, or one can stay home and work around the house, read, or indulge in some other satisfying activity. The person who refrains from visiting the stores will find that he or she is just as happy having stayed at home and having spent nothing on impulse items. Impulse spending does not provide the degree of happiness one might think it would—and it eliminates at least a part of income that might go into building capital.

5. Money burns a hole in one's pocket. Often the individual who carries money seems driven to spend it. This is a strong tendency that must be controlled or redirected to achieve a saving. We will suggest some ways in which this tendency can be controlled or directed into other channels.

6. Most people have very little idea of where their money goes and whether any of their income could have gone into savings. They know how much their paycheck is worth, and they also know that at the end of the period that the paycheck is supposed to cover they have no money left. They may even have to wait a bit to pay bills at the end of the period until the new paycheck arrives. They often do not make an effort to analyze how much they spend and on what.

7. Budgeting for most families is nonexistent. The concept is hardly known. Those who do know the meaning of budgeting have reasons for not employing it. To some it seems to "put life in a straitjacket" and eliminate the joy of living. Actually, budgeting eliminates very little fun, requires little time, and has a good deal of importance if one wishes to save money.

8. Herd instinct and peer pressure are responsible for much overspending in relation to income. Families tend to form into social groups, and individuals join sports and recreation groups which, while they may benefit the members, are hardly conducive to the discipline, the planning, and the study required to build wealth. Group social activities take up a great deal of time and money—drinks with the neighbors each week, dinner with friends every two weeks, and similar pastimes. Playing golf every Saturday takes up the major part of a day, involves buying drinks and perhaps lunch or dinner, and requires the payment of club dues and other fees. At the end of a vigorous social week one is not only fatigued but considerably poorer and less able to build a fund of wealth. Wealth-building is, perhaps unfortunately, something of a "loner" activity.

Rate yourself on expenditures

A most useful experience for all members of the family is to note all expenditures to determine where the money goes each month. This is easily accomplished by supplying a small expense booklet to each member of the family to record each outlay. For those who work outside their home there should be column headings for breakfast, lunch, dinner, postage, bus, taxi, telephone and telegraph, tips, entertainment, repairs, gas and oil, parking, and road tolls. There also should be many blank spaces for write-ins. The person carrying such a booklet should record every cent he or she spends during the month.

The person who pays the household bills will also require columns in which to record outlays for housing, utilities, fuel, telephone, food, clothing, maintenance and repair services, dentist, physician, medication, education, books, transportation, church, charities, laundry and dry cleaning, entertainment, vacations, household supplies, furniture and equipment replacements, auto expenses, insurance, and taxes.

In order to arrive at a realistic total of one's expenditures it is necessary to prorate annual, quarterly, or other periodic payments, such as for life and health insurance, auto insurance, home insurance, property taxes, and even income taxes, as all these must be met out of income.

When the monthly expenditures are added up, the total will almost certainly produce a tremendous shock. An analysis should then be made to see exactly where the fault lies—or rather where the possibilities for saving lie. Entertainment may turn out to be a big item, since it may include dinner out, dinner parties at home, hired help, liquor consumed, and cleanup expenses.

Travel and vacations may turn out to be far more costly than realized, particularly if one uses a charge card and forgets what the item of expense was by the time the bill arrives.

Lunches and drinks in connection with one's job may turn out to be a huge item. One man had a restaurant expense of at least $20 each working day for lunch with a friend or business associate. This daily item amounted to about $5,000 a year. This same man also was inclined to park his car overtime on New York City streets. His fines for one year totaled nearly $6,500.

Simple items such as wines and cigarettes can amount to a large expenditure when one has a $3 bottle of wine with dinner every night, for a total of over $1,000 a year. Even a 65-cent pack of cigarettes each day costs $237 a year.

Impulse buying can cost thousands of dollars per year—for linen napkins, an outdoor grill, new curtains, and on and on.

Whatever the total for the month turns out to be, it will be a revelation—and a first step in controlling expenditures.

From here the policy can be developed of carrying an expense booklet at all times and recording every item of expenditure. Making monthly totals and categorizing expenses will help considerably in the effort to cut costs.

Such a booklet can be useful for other purposes as well. For example, recording in it deductible expenditures, such as subscriptions to investment advisory services, provides a record which can be used to prepare one's income tax return at the end of the year.

Controllable versus noncontrollable expenses

Certain expenses are subject to economies. Others are not, or lend themselves less to economizing. One of the most important things to do, in order to see where expenses can be trimmed, is to separate them into groups.

Relatively uncontrollable expenses are the following:
1. Income taxes—federal, state, and perhaps city
2. Mortgage payments or rent
3. Property taxes
4. Home and/or contents insurance premiums
5. Life insurance premiums
6. Health insurance premiums
7. Pension and/or retirement plan contributions

There is an intermediate category lying between these fixed expenses and controllable outlays. It includes:
1. Food
2. Household supplies
3. Electricity, gas, and water
4. Home repairs and maintenance
5. Car repairs and maintenance
6. Commuting or local transportation expenses in connection with work
7. Education expenses for children
8. Club fees and dues

The group of controllable expenditures includes the following:
1. Eating and drinking at restaurants, bars, and clubs
2. Tickets for movies, stage productions, and sports events
3. Vacations and other trips
4. Liquor and tobacco
5. Items bought on impulse
6. Driving around, stopping to eat and making miscellaneous small purchases

To budget or not to budget

The first step in controlling expenditure is to identify expenses in detail and at all times. Monthly expense booklets are used by many people who wish to make the wisest use of their income. Among those who recommend such booklets is a highly successful banker who has accumulated several business enterprises in addition to occupying his position as bank president. He keeps an expense booklet in which he records every expenditure—even the purchase of a newspaper or shoelaces.

After a short period of filling in the expense booklets the task becomes an easy habit. The simple act of recording every expenditure in itself acts as a control on spending. In a sense it is the opposite of charging a lunch or dinner on your charge card so you do not have to deplete the cash in your wallet.

Totaling expenditures each month acts as a brake on spending. When the size of expenditure is determined after the end of each month the total is generally so large that one is induced immediately to thumb through the book to locate the cause of the "trouble." The result is often a resolve to do better the next month—and the resolve usually contributes to control.

Budgets can, of course, be established for each category of expenditure against which to match actual monthly outgo, but this system may be quite onerous. Also, conventional budgeting assumes that the current level should be the starting point, which should not necessarily be the case. It may be better to use the zero-base budgeting system, now popular in business and in government, requiring justification for every category of outlay in its entirety for each period in the future.

Control of personal expenditures is more the elimination of bad spending habits and the development of good ones than the setting up of detailed budgets against which to measure actual outlays.

Big items and fixed items

Theoretically the big expense items are not controllable. Tax and mortgage payments seem relatively fixed. Actually they may not be.

At the beginning of the 1973-74 recession this writer was in possession of a large house with relatively high fixed expenses. The forecasts of the course of the recession did not give him any feeling of confidence or security for the remainder of the depressed business period.

Houses in the area were not selling well at the time, as might be expected. On the other hand, renting the house was a real possibility.

This was the expense setup of the house at the time a

decision was made to "do something about the big fixed expenses":

Property taxes were about $4,500 a year. Insurance was $1,000. The grounds maintenance was $1,500 and the pool maintenance about the same amount. Gas for heating and cooking was $2,000 a year. Electricity, including air conditioning, was $300. The water bill was about $200. Repairs cost around $4,000 a year. There was no mortgage on the house and thus no mortgage payments. Still, the total of the above expenses came to $15,000 a year.

When the real estate agent appeared with a prospective tenant for the house the contract was quickly drawn up at a rental of $2,200 per month—$26,400 per year.

This writer, as owner of the house, was still responsible for a number of expenses, including property taxes of $4,500 and insurance of $1,000. In addition, he bore $1,000 worth of the pool expense and the entire gardening fee of $1,500 per year. He also paid for half of the repairs—$2,000 instead of $4,000, as a rough figure. He bore $10,000 worth of expenses rather than $15,000 worth. He thus saved $5,000 in expenses and in addition received an annual income of $26,400 from the rental. His "cash flow" was thus better by $5,000 plus $26,400, or $31,400 in all. The picture was even a little better than this because $5,500 of the house expenses were deductible as business expenses since the house was now a commercial proposition. The $4,500 in taxes were always deductible from income before the income tax was computed, even when the house was occupied by this owner. By renting the house, the entire $10,000 worth of expenses became deductible from income before the income tax was computed. Thus, for a person in the 50 percent tax bracket the tax burden was half of $10,000, or just $5,000.

Out of the improved cash flow resulting from the rent of $26,400 plus the saving in expenses of $5,000, new living accommodations had to be paid for, however. These new quarters turned out to be a furnished apartment in Washington, D.C., at a very modest rental. The saving in expenses plus the income from renting the house could have easily supported the rental of an apartment costing ten times as much.

Some people might be startled by the change in "life style" and how this property owner's "living standard" was reduced by moving from a fine large house to an inexpensive apartment.

The life style or living standard may have been cut a bit, but on the other hand perhaps not, as there was enough cash left over from the house rental to provide three months in Europe each summer, still leaving a good deal of money to go into savings. In any event, since the rental was occasioned to a degree by the recession, money worries were eliminated, and peace of mind can be worth a tremendous amount.

Any major expense problem should be hit hard. In the case of this writer, the house was a major item of expense, and something could be done about it.

For the twelve executives in the $70,000-per-year category, previously mentioned, travel was a big item of cash outgo. The answer is simple in a case such as this: Travel less or don't travel at all. If one must travel, go on a week's all-expenses-included tour for $700 for a couple, and not for a few days in the Bahamas for $4,500.

Anyone who feels that such thriftiness would be degrading should bear in mind that some of the richest people are extremely careful about spending money. J. Paul Getty, for example, watched his expenditures like a hawk. At one time he wanted to build a small house in Tulsa, Oklahoma, so that he would have a home near his aircraft factory there. Instead of buying a piece of land on which to build the house, he built it on the grounds of the factory. And by garaging his car inside the factory he avoided the expense of building a garage at his new home.

Guides to controlling expenditures

You may find it helpful to follow these tips for cutting expenses:

1. Do not try to justify large items such as expensive houses and luxury cars on the basis of a "carefully worked out budget" which will cover all items of expenditure and "leave $300 a month to add to savings." It won't work out that way. New expense items crop up. Income goes down. There has to be a large margin between income and outgo in order to provide any assurance of systematic savings. Such "carefully worked out budgets" are little more than attempts to justify extravagances.

2. Buy major assets that go up in value, or at least that do not go down in value. Such items might be a house that is likely to appreciate more than the other houses you are considering, a classic but usable car, and antiques instead of new furniture.

3. Do not eliminate, but try to cut down on, group activities that involve regular and large expenditures such as club dues, entertaining at a club or at restaurants, and giving elaborate parties at home for large groups.

4. Do not go window-shopping. You will usually end up by buying—and often buying things for which you have little or no use or which do not provide satisfaction commensurate with the cash outlay.

5. Carry little cash with you. If you do not carry a great deal of cash you are not likely to find things on which to spend it.

6. Try not to use charge cards. You will then immediately feel exactly what your fun costs you.

7. Try a drastic cutback on liquor and tobacco purchases, or cut them out entirely for a limited period of time. Then see how much you have saved. Try entertaining at Sunday brunch or tea without alcoholic drinks. See what you save, and note whether the guests were less happy than when they have been served liquor.

8. Try out the "multiple purchase theory." See how much a bottle of wine costs you, for instance. Then multiply it by two bottles a week or a bottle for each evening meal. A $3 bottle of wine is certainly not expensive, but a $3 bottle of wine 300 nights a year amounts to $900 just for wine.

9. Remember that you get a certain "kick" out of spending. This is the experience of having money burn a hole in your pocket. You may be able to control this impulse to a degree, thus taking a step toward developing better spending habits. Or you can avoid looking at things that are likely to tempt you. Or you can buy assets that may appreciate in value—and still get the same satisfaction from spending. You can buy antique furniture, or old glass and china, or antique silver, even a piece that costs $10. The satisfaction of spending is there, but one asset is exchanged for another, and the asset purchased to satisfy the spending urge may very well appreciate in value and thus prove to be a good investment.

10. Find activities other than those involving expenditures to take up your spare time. Work in the garden, work on your car, exercise, visit museums, develop an expert knowledge of art or antiques with which, incidentally, you might very well make a good deal of money.

11. Get out of the "executive lunch club" in which each lunch costs you $5 or more plus drinks plus the lunch of the person who is your guest. You may well find that going to lunch with business associates is not essential to business success. Try the counter lunch or lunch in the office. Again, multiply your savings per working day of, say, $5 by five days a week, or even three days a week, for fifty weeks and see what your savings are per year.

12. If you want to engage in "conspicuous consumption and emulation" to impress your friends and business associates, try buying art and antiques as investments and filling your home with them. Try buying—and selling—a home as an investment. Try buying a car that will go up

in value and not down—like a Rolls-Royce that has proven over the past three years, including the recent recession, to be one of the best investments. If you do not want to incur repairs on this investment, buy a four-cylinder economy car for everyday use. The Rolls-Royce will be impressive no matter how much or how little you use it.

13. Keep firmly in mind the fact that right now, today, the satisfactions that you got out of spending yesterday are gone. There is no carryover or carry forward; but there would be a carry forward of savings and capital.

14. Friends and business associates are fine to have, and sharing leisure activities with them provides satisfactions for you and your family; but so does a fund of capital provide satisfactions. You will find that a little economy and a little absence of yourself and your family from some of the more costly social get-togethers will lose far fewer of your friends than you thought.

CHAPTER 4

Wealth Through Saving

In 1961 a hypothetical savings plan was prepared for Olive Smith, age forty-five, who wanted to determine to what extent such a plan could build up her capital during the remainder of her working life. If the results seemed worthwhile, she would try to follow the plan.

It showed that by January 1, 1977, she would have accumulated savings of $75,829, on which she would receive monthly interest of $758.29. By January 1, 1980, when the plan would end, she would have accumulated $108,476 in capital and would be receiving a monthly interest payment of $1,084.76—$13,017.12 a year.

But Olive Smith (not the real name, but a real saver as well as a real person) did even better than the theoretical savings plan. As of 1976 she had accumulated well over $200,000 and had annual income exceeding $20,000. Of course there were other sources of income, mostly from a government pension, but interest income on the capital amounted in 1976 to about $15,000. This is not the best return that might have been secured on $200,000, but this saver chose minimum-risk government notes as her main investment.

Olive Smith began with an investment in a corporate note which yielded exactly 12 percent per annum. Compounding was done monthly by the corporation so that the annual yield was a little over 12 percent. Sometimes a return as low as 10 percent had to be taken during the years covered by the plan. Sometimes, as in 1973 and even later, returns of over 12 percent were quite common, and capital was relatively safe in the United States or abroad.

The savings plan of $200 a month, invested after taxes had been paid, seemed to set an entirely possible goal for Olive Smith. She and her husband both worked, although neither received a high salary.

On January 1, 1961, she invested $1,000 in the plan, and at the end of the month the interest she earned amounted to $10—1 percent per month, or 12 percent per year compounded monthly.

Olive left this $10 in the account in order to earn interest, so that her monthly savings for the second month were her $200 plus the $10 she had reinvested. The interest on this total capital during the following month was $12.10—1 percent of $1,210.

At the end of one year, including her investment of $200 made as of January 1, 1962, she had invested a total of $3,400; interest earned and reinvested made this total grow to $3,662.

In the normal course of events her salary would probably increase, and her husband could expect raises in his government job. They did not, however, plan to raise the $200 monthly investment allocation. As income goes up so do taxes, and they felt it would be hard to increase the

Your Race with Inflation

In 1965	In 1975	In 1985
If you had this income	*You needed this income to be as well off*	*You will need this income to be as well off if inflation continues to average 5.5% annually*
$ 5,000	$ 8,723	$ 16,029
$ 7,500	$ 13,444	$ 24,459
$ 10,000	$ 17,831	$ 32,781
$ 15,000	$ 27,159	$ 51,629
$ 20,000	$ 36,706	$ 71,619
$ 25,000	$ 46,728	$ 91,071
$ 30,000	$ 57,193	$109,721
$ 35,000	$ 67,600	$127,486
$ 40,000	$ 77,583	$144,526
$ 50,000	$ 96,383	$176,617
$100,000	$177,884	$315,741
$250,000	$377,921	$657,203

Note: Figures are for a married couple with two children and take into account federal but not state and local taxes. It is assumed that income is all from wages and salaries and that prices will rise nearly 71 percent between 1975 and 1985, as they did between 1965 and 1975.

Source: *U.S.News & World Report*

monthly saving of $200. Also, it did not seem necessary because $200 a month saved under the plan would achieve their goal of enough capital plus enough monthly income from the capital after both of them retired from work.

Even at the present rate of inflation the original goal worked out in 1961 still looks good—capital of $108,476 in a period of nineteen years and a monthly income of $1,084.76. After the plan was initiated, however, the monthly savings were increased and the goal was achieved much sooner. Although their income rose, they continued to live modestly, travel inexpensively, entertain simply, and occupy the same low-cost apartment they had rented in the 1950s.

A savings plan

If you wish to build wealth through savings, as Olive Smith did, the plan shown on pages 60-61 may serve as a guide to the development of your own program. When you consult this hypothetical savings plan, remember that an annual return of 12 percent on the invested funds is necessary if the plan is to work.

By the end of 1983 the individual using this plan will accumulate $22,986 and will receive monthly interest of $229.86 on a total investment of $15,400. But by that time the tax burden will be so great that it may not be possible to save as much as before, or even to save at all. However, the individual need no longer save anything. All that is necessary is to allow interest to accumulate in the account and to pay the tax on it. From then on, the savings account will, of course, grow more slowly since $200 will not be added to it each month.

By 1997, on retirement at age sixty-five, the saver will have capital of $108,476—on total savings of $15,400 put into the plan. The monthly interest check will amount to $1,084.76. Of course this income will be in addition to any pension or annuity payments received.

Multiplying your capital

At a rate of 1 percent per month, or 12 percent per year compounded monthly, capital doubles in six years and quadruples in twelve years—that is, if taxes are not deducted or if tax on the income from the savings fund is paid out of income from some other source, such as one's salary or fees as a self-employed professional.

Thus $10,000 placed in a savings fund at 12 percent per year compounded monthly becomes $20,000 in six years and $40,000 in twelve years. The 12 percent per annum rate is used here as it has been a "target rate" for this investor for the past twenty years. It was a rate to try to achieve each year. Sometimes one had to settle for 10 percent instead of 12 percent, but this was offset by rates higher than 12 percent in many years, including the high interest era of 1973-74 as well as 1976, when some extremely high international rates were available.

Large amounts of capital can also be built up by those who qualify to use one of the remarkable savings opportunities made possible by the Self-Employed Individuals Tax Retirement Act of 1962, known as the Keogh Plan, and the Employee Retirement Income Security Act of 1974, which permits Individual Retirement Accounts. These two plans could very well revolutionize savings by individuals in the United States.

Individual Retirement Accounts

Any person under the age of seventy and one-half who receives wages or a salary from an employer or from self-employment and is not covered by a qualified pension or retirement plan can set up an Individual Retirement Account (IRA).

This category includes any employee who does not wish to join his or her employer's qualified plan.

The essence of such a plan is that an individual can save 15 percent of earned income—not investment income— up to a maximum of $1,500 annually, and the entire

Savings Program for an Individual Age 45
($1,000 Initial Investment at 12% per Year; Savings at Rate of $200 per Month)

Date	Periodic Saving	Total Savings Put Into Plan	Interest on Total Investment - 1% Per Month	New Balance of Total Investment
Jan. 1, 1978	$1,000	$1,000		
Feb. 1	200	1,200	$10.00	$1,210
March 1	200	1,400	12.10	1,422
April 1	200	1,600	14.22	1,636
May 1	200	1,800	16.36	1,852
June 1	200	2,000	18.52	2,070
July 1	200	2,200	20.70	2,291
Aug. 1	200	2,400	22.91	2,514
Sept. 1	200	2,600	25.14	2,739
Oct. 1	200	2,800	27.39	2,966
Nov. 1	200	3,000	29.66	3,196
Dec. 1	200	3,200	31.96	3,428
Jan. 1, 1979	200	3,400	34.28	3,662
Jan. 1, 1980	200	5,800	63.99	6,663
Jan. 1, 1981	200	8,200	97.48	10,045
Jan. 1, 1982	200	10,600	135.20	13,855
Jan. 1, 1983	200	13,000	177.71	18,149

Savings Program for an Individual Age 52
(1984 to Retirement in 1997 at Age 65;
No Savings - Only Reinvestment of
12% Annual Interest)

Date	New Balance of Total Investment	Monthly Interest
Jan. 1, 1984	$22,986	$229.86
Jan. 1, 1985	25,900	259.00
Jan. 1, 1986	29,184	291.84
Jan. 1, 1987	32,884	328.84
Jan. 1, 1988	37,053	370.53
Jan. 1, 1989	41,750	417.50
Jan. 1, 1990	47,043	470.43
Jan. 1, 1991	53,007	. 530.07
Jan. 1, 1992	59,727	597.27
Jan. 1, 1993	67,298	672.98
Jan. 1, 1994	75,829	758.29
Jan. 1, 1995	85,442	854.42
Jan. 1, 1996	96,273	962.73
Jan. 1, 1997	108,476	1,084.76

amount saved each year can be subtracted from income before the federal income tax is computed.

There is no tax on the amount saved, and there is no tax on the earnings of the fund until it is drawn down on retirement. Then tax is paid on the amount withdrawn, but by then the individual is likely to be in a lower tax bracket than during the years when the money was earned.

The annual savings can be put into a bank account or a savings and loan account; or, with a bank acting as custodian, the funds can be placed in stocks, bonds, or any other medium of investment. Another possibility is to use the savings to buy an annuity-type policy from an insurance company.

The individual can retire and begin to withdraw the IRA funds (and pay tax on the withdrawals) any time after age fifty-nine and one-half, but must start withdrawing funds on reaching age seventy and one-half. Withdrawals made before age fifty-nine and one-half are subject to income tax and there is also a tax penalty of 10 percent on the amount withdrawn. If the individual becomes permanently disabled, early withdrawals are not subject to the 10 percent penalty.

Many banks have established plans for the deposit of IRA funds in savings accounts. For annual contributions up to $500, the interest rate in early 1977 was about 5.25 percent. As interest was compounded daily, the effective annual yield was 5.47 percent. Annual contributions of $500 to $1,000 earned an annual interest rate of 6.75 percent, which by compounding worked out to 7.08 per year. Annual deposits of $1,000 to $1,500 earned at the top rate of 7.75 percent, which when compounded yielded 8.17 percent annually. It must be emphasized that rates of interest can, and most certainly do, change from time to time.

The amounts that can be accumulated under such a plan can be substantial. This is a table issued by a New

York savings bank in early 1977 to show how capital builds up at an interest rate of 7.75 percent per year:

If You Start an IRA Plan at Age	Total Amount You Deposit	Interest Earned	Total Savings at Age 65
25	$60,000	$380,044	$440,044
30	52,500	238,141	290,641
35	45,000	144,773	189,773
40	37,500	84,174	121,674
50	22,500	22,157	44,657
60	7,500	2,052	9,552

In 1977 a new provision was added to IRAs for the benefit of homemakers: If only the husband or the wife receives earned income, he or she may contribute a maximum of $1,750 to a special joint account.

An important feature of IRAs is that if a company pension fund goes out of existence or if an employee leaves a company, the accumulated sum received from the company pension fund can be put in an Individual Retirement Account without having to pay tax—no matter how large the sum. It is reported that some laid-off business executives have put as much as $400,000 into their IRAs in this manner. There the money can remain and earn until at age fifty-nine and one-half to seventy and one-half the individual begins withdrawing from the fund. But as withdrawals are made, the balance in the account continues to earn interest until all the money is drawn out.

Keogh plan only for the self-employed

The Keogh plan offers self-employed individuals an opportunity to accumulate a fund of wealth which, upon retirement, can be paid to them in a lump sum or over a period of time. As with IRAs, savings institutions of var-

The Increase in Keogh Plans
With Life Insurance Companies

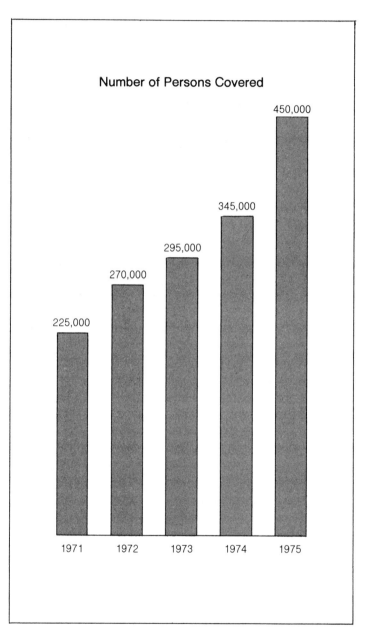

Number of Persons Covered

				450,000
			345,000	
		295,000		
	270,000			
225,000				
1971	1972	1973	1974	1975

Source: American Council of Life Insurance

ious kinds place the funds on deposit or invest them. Also as in the case of IRAs, only earned income, not invest-ment income, is eligible for the plan.

Under the Keogh plan an individual can place as much as 15 percent of earned income, to a maximum of $7,500 a year, in a personal retirement fund. If the adjusted gross income of the self-employed person does not exceed $15,000, then the sum of $750 or 100 percent of the in-come, whichever is less, can be put in the fund, regard-less of the 15 percent limitation.

The annual amount put into a Keogh plan can be de-ducted from income before computing the federal in-come tax. Thus, if the individual is in the 50 percent tax bracket, 50 percent of $7,500—$3,750—is saved (or at least tax-deferred) every year that a $7,500 investment is made in the plan.

One feature that makes a Keogh plan even more at-tractive to the high-income person is that the $7,500 an-nual maximum contribution can be increased by $2,500 or 10 percent of annual income, whichever is lower. This additional contribution of up to $2,500 is not tax-deduct-ible from income in the year in which it is placed in the fund; but the earnings on it are not taxed as they accumu-late. From this point of view they have the same pre-ferred tax status as the original maximum contribution of $7,500.

There is, however, one possible disadvantage in estab-lishing a Keogh plan. If the self-employed person has em-ployees, the plan must include them, and their employer must contribute on their behalf to the plan. For this rea-son, some self-employed persons may prefer to set up In-dividual Retirement Accounts, which do not require contributions for employees.

As in the case of an IRA, interest earned in a Keogh plan is not taxed. Only withdrawals are taxed, and payouts must start between the ages of fifty-nine and one-half and seventy and one-half. Payouts can be in lump sum or spread over ten years. If the withdrawal is in a lump sum, it is taxed as though it were spread over ten years, an income-averaging procedure. Tax savings under this option can be substantial. Although withdrawal must begin by age seventy and one-half, it is possible to continue working past that age and earn an income while receiving payouts from a Keogh plan.

Even part-time self-employed individuals can use a Keogh plan. An example is an accountant who is a full-time company employee but also prepares statements and income tax returns for various clients in the evenings and weekends. The income from his self-employment is eligible for a Keogh plan.

A person with an annual self-employment income of, say, $10,000 can put up to 15 percent of this amount into a Keogh plan. Thus, the individual who begins contributing this 15 percent, or $1,500, at age thirty and continues the plan to age sixty-five will have contributed $52,500. But interest at current savings bank levels for six-to-seven-year accounts at 7.75 percent per annum compounded daily will add $238,141. At age sixty-five the total fund will amount to $290,641. This can be withdrawn in a lump sum or there can be a ten-year payout, in which case the balance remaining in the account after each payment continues to earn interest. At the end of ten years the total payout should, through accumulation of interest on the balance, amount to $423,356—a healthy sum to have accumulated by making an annual contribution to the fund of $1,500 per year, or $125 per month.

At the other end of the permitted contribution scale is the self-employed person with an annual income of $50,000 who can contribute $7,500 a year from age thirty to age sixty-five, when the saver begins to draw down the fund. The total amount contributed to the funds is $262,500, but the accumulated interest is $1,190,707, making a total distributable fund at age sixty-five of $1,453,207. This sum can be paid out over ten years at the rate of $211,678 a year, and payouts can be received quarterly. By the time the fund is paid out and interest on the remaining balance has ended, the participant in the plan will have received $2,116,780.

To be more realistic than citing a thirty-year-old who can accumulate over $2 million by the age of sixty-five, there are self-employed people who, at age forty-two, earn $50,000 and are thus eligible to put $7,500 into the plan each year. These individuals can accumulate $505,473 by the age of sixty-five.

The person earning $25,000 a year who at age forty-two begins putting the maximum permissible ($3,750) into the plan annually will have accumulated $252,737 by age sixty-five.

It should be borne in mind that the above projections are based on 1977 interest rates for six-to-seven-year accounts. If future rates are lower, the capital buildup will be less. If the rates are higher, the buildup can be much greater or much sooner.

5

A Home
as an
Investment

One of the greatest opportunities for building wealth results from the fact that a home can be an appreciating investment.

Since the main objective in homeownership is to have a place in which to live and to bring up one's family, if appreciation in value does not take place as anticipated, all is not lost by any means. The investment aspect of a home is an "added feature."

These are some of the reasons why one's home can be not only a good investment but one's best investment:

1. A home is the most mortgageable of all real estate. There is no shortage of banks and savings and loan associations that stand ready on a day's notice to make a loan on a marketable property to a person with reasonably good

credit. If a large mortgage cannot be obtained, a smaller one can be secured in almost every case.

2. Houses have been appreciating fairly steadily. In fact the price rise in the last fifteen years has probably been greater than in any other fifteen-year period in the history of the United States.

3. In the last three years, houses have appreciated in many areas even faster than for the entire fifteen-year period. This has been the case in Washington, D.C., and its suburbs, in the suburbs of New York City, and in Tucson, Arizona, as just a few examples.

4. The greatest appreciation in value has taken place in the past three years in less expensive houses, so that appreciation has been available to a tremendous group of people able to afford only modest homes.

5. Taxes are very much slanted in favor of the homeowner. The instructions for Form 1040, issued by the Internal Revenue Service, summarize the tax rule briefly but completely:

> Sale of Personal Residence. - Tax on a portion or all of the gain from the sale of your principal residence must be deferred if:
> (1) within 18 months after or before the sale, you purchase another principal residence and use it as such; or
> (2) before the sale or within 18 months after the sale, you begin construction of a new principal residence and use it as such not later than two years after the sale.

No matter how many principal residences you buy and sell, if you use all the money received for your old home to purchase another home, you do not pay tax on the profit on each home sold. The tax *must* be deferred.

A case study
Home Number One
In January 1956 we saw a house in Washington, D.C., with a prominently displayed "For Sale" sign on it. We had noticed the house several times before when driving

by it. It was located on Florida Avenue near Massachusetts Avenue. The color was what caught our eye each time. The house was painted a very definite purple.

Although the color might have precluded the sale of the house to others, it fascinated us. The house had been recently renovated. Prior to its purple phase it had been red brick with an arched doorway—a Victorian-style house constructed at the turn of the century.

In 1956 the house was, however, eminently up to date. It had a new squared-off doorway, gray-white trim, black shutters, and a paneled front door. It was a distinctly Georgetown-type house, in advance of "the gaslight look" which shortly thereafter seemed to sweep the country. It was the only such house on the block. Across the street were two large, solid-looking brick houses. The other houses in the area were run-down. Diagonally across the street was a condemned apartment house with a large chain and padlock on the front door.

Nevertheless we found the purple house intriguing and its in-town location quite convenient, so we rang the bell. The seller was an employee of a real estate firm who had bought the house in its original Victorian state and modernized it in order to make a profit on resale. Since he was a maintenance man he was particularly concerned with the heating system, the wiring, the plumbing, the bathrooms, and the kitchen. The bathrooms and the kitchen were new and the heating system had been converted from coal to oil and was in excellent working order.

The house was of unusual design. On each of the four floors there were two rooms. There was a bathroom between the second and third floors and another bathroom between the third and fourth floors.

An interior decorator had been retained to redecorate the house completely and had coordinated the paint, wallpaper, and fixtures.

The asking price was $18,500. We knew from a study of house values in Washington that this was a low price for a

completely modernized eight-room house with two
baths, but we also knew that the street was not a good
one and that the padlocked apartment house across the
street indicated a generally poor area.

Next to the purple house was a rooming house. Across
the street was another rooming house and on the corner
was a third. The last was of the era of the purple house
before its restoration and modernization.

On the other hand, we knew that just around the
corner was an excellent street with houses worth $40,000,
$50,000, and even $100,000. And the purple house was
not quite two blocks away from Massachusetts Avenue,
one of Washington's best thoroughfares.

About ten minutes after entering the purple house we
made an offer of $17,500. The seller was reluctant to ac-
cept it. From his conversation, however, it was obvious
that he had been offering the house for sale for a long
time without success and that he was getting tired of the
whole project.

The seller told us that the house warranted a mortgage
of $12,000 and that if our offer were to be accepted we
would have to make a down payment of $5,500. He
seemed to expect us to answer that we could not make a
down payment of this size; but fortunately we could. That
clinched the deal. We had the house for $17,500.

The purple house was the most economical we have
ever owned. The mortgage payments, including interest
and amortization, amounted to $117.50 a month. Taxes
were an almost unbelievably low $120 a year because the
house was on a very small, irregularly shaped piece of
land that had little value. The heating bill ran up to $79
in the coldest month but was usually around $60 during
the winter.

At the end of three years we sold the house at a net
profit to us of $11,000 after we had paid the real estate
agent's sales commission—a profit of over 62 percent on
the original purchase price of $17,500.

The maximum investment on our part was the down payment of $5,500 plus another $2,000 that we paid on the mortgage—$7,500 in all. The profit represented almost 150 percent on this $7,500 investment. Of course, when we sold the house we had to pay off the remaining balance of the mortgage—$10,000.

How was a profit of this size possible?

First, the neighborhood changed for the better. It is sometimes difficult to assess whether a borderline neighborhood is moving up or down. The most important single factor was the sale and complete rehabilitation of the old padlocked apartment house across the street from us.

Our house was among the first "Georgetown lamp-in-front" painted bricks. This type of rehabilitation took place in other houses on our block as well as in other areas of Washington. The rooming house next to us was repainted and two of the older houses across the street were painted. Only a certain number of houses on any street need to be rehabilitated before the entire neighborhood moves upward; and our street was an ugly duckling between two excellent streets.

Home Number Two

After we sold the purple house we were $11,000 better off than we were when we owned it, and we began to look for a better house in a better neighborhood. On one of the very best residential streets in Washington we found the most run-down house we had ever seen. It was located on the corner of Connecticut and Wyoming Avenues. We felt that the corner site was very valuable.

The house had once been the fine residence of a senator. During World War II it had been converted for use as an apartment house. In the years 1940 to 1945 Washington was overflowing with government workers and representatives of industry who wanted to do business with the government. The huge demand for living space resulted in some impossible conversions of private homes to apartments, and the house on the corner of Connecticut and Wyoming Avenues seemed the most impossible of all. Closets and partitions had been flimsily constructed, and sinks had been installed in most of the one-room "apartments."

This jerry-built apartment house had deteriorated so much since the war that it was almost vacant. As an apartment building it was a losing proposition. It was owned by a group of heirs of the original owner, and they were interested in nothing so much as getting rid of the building for any face-saving sum. There was, however, a minor heir and the court had jurisdiction. The court secured three remarkably close appraisals on the property and we offered something less than these appraisals. Three months after we made our offer we were in possession of the house—for $28,000. This was approximately what we had received for our first house. There was thus no tax to pay on the profit from the sale of the purple house.

Our "new" house required an enormous amount of rehabilitation. The plaster on the walls and ceilings of nine of its ten rooms had disintegrated beyond repair. We removed all of the plaster down to the bricks and took out all of the partitions that had been used to convert the original house to apartments. The replastering job lasted seven months and cost about $7,000. We rewired the house and installed new partitions and fixtures, two new baths, and a new kitchen. A good deal of the woodwork had deteriorated badly. It took an additional month to complete the necessary carpentry and several more weeks to have the interior painted. The floors needed refinishing, but there was enough good hardwood left to allow sanding and revarnishing. At that point we had a completely new interior.

It might seem that this property offered little other than a big opportunity to spend money; but basically the house was sound. The foundations were excellent; the wood was free from termites; and the structural members between the floors were in good condition. The outside was of fine glazed brick, and the cement between the bricks had not deteriorated.

The exterior bricks we painted beige. We tore out the stone handrail that was beside the steps leading from the front door to the front walk and replaced it with an iron grillwork rail. We installed a series of small glass panes in the windows above the front door in place of the large panes. In front of these windows we placed an iron grill-work box for flowers.

In front of the house we installed two large lanterns on wrought-iron poles. The front porch, the steps, and the walkway to the street we paved with flagstones as a replacement for the concrete. We converted the glass-paneled front door to one containing a series of wood panels trimmed with raised wood borders.

Throughout the house we installed large modern brass doorknobs with large flat backing plates. We also installed modern one-button electric switches and new lighting fixtures, including fixtures of Venetian glass and metal.

As finishing touches we installed black and white tile on the first floor, floor-to-ceiling curtains to match the walls throughout the house, and extensive wall-to-wall carpeting.

In all, we spent $17,000 for rehabilitation, which when added to the $28,000 purchase price made an investment of $45,000.

We lived in the house for a year and a half and then sold it to a foreign government for use as its chancery— for $76,000. The profit after the real estate agent's commission was $27,000.

At this point we had two profits to add together, $11,000 on the first house and $27,000 on the second, $38,000 in all.

Why did Home Number Two bring so much money so quickly? In the first place it was tastefully restored from dilapidation to what at the time was up-to-date perfection. Also, the house was transformed from Victorian to "Federal-type Georgetown," the architecture in vogue at the time.

There were, however, other elements present which were just as important to the house's ultimate value, perhaps even more so. The house was on a strategic and very valuable corner. Diagonally across the street was the apartment house known as "2101 Connecticut Avenue." This was not a new apartment house but in it lived some of the most prominent people in Washington.

On one side of our house was Connecticut Avenue, an excellent thoroughfare, and on the other Wyoming Avenue, sometimes known as "Washington's Gold Coast." The house we bought was the one eyesore in the neighborhood. After the transformation it became one of the most attractive houses in the area, and its excellent room arrangement and convenient location made it eminently suitable for use as the chancery of a foreign government.

Home Number Three

At the time we sold our second house it became necessary for us to move to the New York City area. Only by studying an area firsthand can house values be fixed in one's mind. For about two months we looked at suburban houses there and read house advertisements in the newspapers every day.

One cold, snowy morning when house-hunting outside the city was difficult, we paid a visit to the Previews real estate firm in New York City and asked to look at brochures about properties in the area around the city. The manager pulled out a brochure on a house that appeared to be exactly what we would want if we could pick an ideal home without regard to cost or maintenance. Despite the snow and cold we made arrangements to visit the house that day.

The house was in the prestige subdivision known as the Crossways in Bronxville, New York. It was the largest and most imposing house in the area and probably the most expensive ever built in Bronxville. It was a grand Elizabethan-style house designed by the eminent architect Louis Bowman and built in 1928 at a cost of $515,000.

The exterior was of Belgian brick. The leaded doors and windows had been imported from England. The living room, thirty-four by twenty-two feet, with molded plaster ceiling, was paneled with French walnut. The dining room, twenty-two by twenty feet, was paneled with carved Hungarian oak. The circular entrance hall had a floor of imported Italian green and white marble and the door fixtures were solid silver. The solarium-breakfast room, thirty-three by sixteen feet, was completely tiled and there was a fountain at one end. Almost throughout the house there were gold-plated fixtures—bath faucets, doorknobs and hinges, and metal trimming of all kinds. The seven baths were tiled in ceramics especially made for the house. The bath fixtures were marble. Throughout the house were new silk curtains of fine design.

There was a circular staircase to the second floor with an ornamental iron stair rail made for the house. The stairwell had a solid silver chandelier and in the ceiling was a map of the heavens in lights, including the Big Dipper. All of the "stars" seemed to twinkle when the electricity was turned on.

In all, the house had eighteen rooms and there was a three-car garage in one of its wings. The house had been owned by an elderly publisher, who had been offered $200,000 for it two years prior to his death. He had turned down the offer and had demanded $300,000.

Upon the demise of the publisher his estate went to his children, all of whom seemed well off. The house, being very large, was not in demand, and at an asking price of $195,000 it failed to find a buyer for a long time. In the meantime the property tax of $5,800 a year—quite a large tax in the early 1960s—had to be paid.

The house did need some repairs to the chimneys, the

brickwork, and the wood beams on the exterior. It also needed new bath fixtures in the "lesser bathrooms" and a new hot water heater. Basically, however, the house and grounds were in good condition.

Our offer that bought the house was $60,000, plus a car worth $5,000 as the commission to the real estate agent. Included with the house were many furnishings, among them a Sarouk carpet, seventeen by twenty-nine feet, apparently made for the living room. At the closing the attorneys produced a bill of sale for the carpet showing that it had cost $8,800!

To the $65,000, or a little less, that the house cost us had to be added $12,000 for repairs, bringing the total invested in the house almost to $77,000, slightly more than we secured from the sale of our previous house. Thus no taxes were due as the entire proceeds of Home Number Two were put into Home Number Three.

One year later we sold Home Number Three for $125,000. After paying the agent's commission, the profit on the house amounted to about $43,000, plus some profit on the Sarouk carpet and a few other furnishings wanted by the foreign government that bought the house.

The profit on this house plus the $38,000 total on Homes Number One and Two amounted to about $81,000.

There were several reasons for our financial success with Home Number Three:

The time of year and the day the house was offered to us were very bad for sales—December and a snowy, sleety day.

The house had been on the market a long time before we bought it.

The heirs looked upon the house as being a white elephant that they no doubt wished would "go away."

The newly created nations that were sending ambassadors to the United Nations needed embassies, and this house could be a palatial embassy. Embassies do not pay property taxes and so the buyer was unconcerned about the heavy taxes on the house.

The house was a forecast of things to come. It was the type of baronial home that has become increasingly popular as affluence has spread in this country.

At the time we bought the house the emphasis was on smaller and less expensive houses. Thus the house was correct for the times and for the trend. Even if the foreign government had not bought it, the house would have sold well, but probably not so quickly and not without financing problems.

Home Number Four

The net receipt from the sale of Home Number Three was about $120,000. If tax were to be avoided, this sum would have to be invested in another home.

Within a year we found a house that we felt would be suitable for us. It was a Georgian-style house on over five acres, directly on the waterfront with its own protected harbor in which one could keep a sailboat, a motor boat, or even a large yacht. The property had a beach and a seawall over 500 feet long.

The house had fifteen rooms and five baths, plus a three-car garage and a greenhouse. The entire house and grounds had just been renovated at a cost of about $150,000 by the owner, an extremely wealthy man. The baths were new; the kitchen and all of its equipment were new; the wiring was new and the very best. The heating system was the most advanced design of the gas hot water baseboard type, with a Bell and Gossett monoflow valve system with five zones. There was an elaborate fire-control system on each floor.

The owner said he wanted to sell the house because he had too many homes and intended to "simplify my existence." He offered the estate, located in Rye, New York, for $175,000.

After turning down a number of offers, he at last accepted $110,000 plus a painting that had cost us $1,400. Our cost was thus $111,400.

Fixing up was required, but not a great deal. Shutters were installed on the windows to add to the attractiveness of the house. Considerable interior and exterior paint work had to be done too. The owner had removed some of the furnishings he liked. He had pulled two large mirrors out of the wall and had taken a bar refrigerator and some other items.

The property in the winter had a most forlorn appearance, particularly the overgrown tennis court. The owner had added a corner lot, consisting of an acre of overgrown gardens and lawns. This acre we improved and maintained as gardens and lawns. There were in all three and a half acres of lawns.

When we finished all of the necessary work we had invested the approximately $120,000 we had received from the sale of Home Number Three.

We bought the house in December 1963. We sold it four years later for a net to us of $210,000 after the real estate agent's selling commission was paid. We had made about $90,000 on the house. This profit plus the profit of $81,000 up to this point amounted to $171,000.

We had been able to buy Home Number Four at a favorable price because the owner was so wealthy and so tired of owning too many homes that he was willing to sacrifice it. Besides, a property with an extensive waterfront and five acres of land was not much wanted at that time. The emphasis then was still on the smaller home with not much land.

We had made the property immaculate and attractive in every way, and we had done this for a reasonable amount of money. But we found it very difficult to sell this house, and were able to do so only after a "run to the suburbs" developed in the mid-1960s because of urban problems. We finally sold the house to a man who had just received a windfall from the sale of stock in his manufacturing company. A person who receives a windfall is not inclined to quibble about the price of something that is desired.

To sum up our real estate investments to this point:

In Home Number One $17,500 was invested. The sales price of $29,000 was the net received. Furniture was sold with this house and the nominal price was $33,000. A profit was realized on the furniture.

The sales price of Home Number One was invested in Home Number Two. This sum was still $17,500 original cash; but $17,000 for the rehabilitation of Home Number Two had to be added, making $34,500 in all.

The selling price of $76,000 for Home Number Two was put into Home Number Three in Bronxville, New York. The sum involved was the $65,000 purchase price plus $12,000 for rehabilitation. We were, however, $1,000 short and this $1,000 had to be added to our "original cash invested to date" of $34,500, making $35,500 in all.

The entire proceeds of Home Number Three were invested in Home Number Four in Rye, New York, including its rehabilitation costs. Thus, at the time we received the $210,000 net for Home Number Four we had invested $35,500 in cash.

Home Number Five

In buying Home Number Five we bought one house too many! We had looked at many houses without finding one we wanted. Then we found Home Number Four in Rye, New York, and placed a bid on it. But we also placed a bid on a large house in Westport, Connecticut, which we felt would suit our purposes. We then waited to see which house, if any, we would get.

The Westport house had eighteen rooms and seven baths. It had been built in the eighteenth century but had been expanded during the first half of the nineteenth century. Early in this century it had been completely re-stored to its Colonial splendor with tall pillars. The rooms were very large and had some Victorian trim, fireplaces, and other features. The top floor was a huge theater. There was a large detached garage and the remnants of a large sunken formal garden that was badly overgrown. The three and three-quarter acres of land sloped down to a small lake. The property was bounded by a fine orna-mental stone and iron fence and lamp posts.

The asking price for the house had been $120,000. There were no bidders and the price had been reduced to $80,000. We looked at the property and then went on with our house-hunting. We later visited a number of homes in Westport with a new real estate agent. The agent drove us onto the grounds of this house that we had already seen. We indicated that we had previously decid-ed against it. At this point the owner appeared and mo-tioned to the real estate agent to come over as he apparently wanted to talk with her confidentially. The real estate agent talked with the owner, then returned to us and said, "The owner is most anxious to sell right now and will consider any reasonable offer."

Our "reasonable offer" was $60,000. After a day of con-sideration the owner indicated that if we would raise the offer to $63,000 the house would be ours. We closed at $63,000. The reason for the forced sale was family prob-lems. Otherwise we doubt whether $63,000 would have purchased the house. This became our Home Number Five although we had just purchased Home Number Four. We now owned two houses at the same time.

The main defect of this house was its decor, which was "shopworn modern" and did not suit the antique style of the architecture. Our task was to restore the house to approximately its original condition. This included clean-ing up the grounds, painting and varnishing the interior, and furnishing it with period antiques to complement its historic appearance.

We did the rehabilitation job, with very little outside help, over a period of three months. Our total cash outlay was $2,550, making a total of $65,550 invested in Home Number Five.

Within one year we sold the house for a net to us of $95,000 after commission to the selling agent. We made nearly $30,000 on an investment of $65,550 in a year. We also sold furniture with the house at something of a profit. We did, however, have to take the trade of a New York apartment on Fifth Avenue overlooking Central Park. We allowed $60,000 for the apartment as a partial payment on Home Number Five. We kept the apartment for a while because in the meantime we had rented out Home Number Four in Rye. After we moved back to Rye, some months later, we sold the apartment for exactly what we had allowed on it—$60,000.

On the $30,000 profit we had to pay a capital gains tax of 25 percent, or $7,500, leaving $22,500 profit after taxes. Perhaps this $22,500 should be subtracted from the $35,500 invested to date in our string of principal residences. Thus, perhaps our real estate transactions cost us $35,500 less $22,500, making a net investment of $13,000.

Home Number Six
Shortly after selling the house in Rye we moved back to Washington, D.C., where this writer took up his post as a professor at American University. One of the things we soon did was to buy a house within walking distance of the university.

Here again the owner was anxious to sell as he had bought another home and did not want to be burdened with two houses. He had been asking $175,000 for the house but was willing to make some concessions.

The house was no standout but it was relatively new— about six years old—and had been constructed by a highly reputable builder. It stood on one of the larger lots on

Loughboro Road, a good residential street far from Washington's problem areas. The house had six bedrooms and seven baths. The basement had been converted to an enormous recreation area with two baths and a powder room. There was central air conditioning and a built-in two-car garage. The land was over half an acre, sizable for the area.

The great deficiency of the house was the lack of finishing touches. One real estate agent remarked that the house looked as if it did not have any eyebrows. The shutters were undecorated and the house seemed drab.

We settled on it—for $130,000, paid by $35,000 cash and an eighteen-month standing mortgage at the rather low rate of 5 percent per annum. Usually mortgage payments are a combination of interest and amortization of the mortgage, but in a standing mortgage only the interest is paid monthly. This kind of mortgage suited us at the time because we wanted to minimize our monthly cash outflow.

We bought the house in the winter, but lost no time in improving it despite the freezing weather. The "no eyebrows" fault we corrected by outlining the shutters and door panels with contrasting paint, and adding wrought-iron window boxes and a wrought-iron fence running the width of the property.

We felt the house should be larger and thus more impressive, and we achieved this effect by extending the line of the end of the house with a curving wall of bricks ending in a brick pillar. The house looked about 25 percent bigger after the wall was completed.

The interior was improved by installing fine new chandeliers, including ones in the modern kitchen and in the paneled bar. We put metallic gold and silver wallpaper on several walls and ceilings, including the wall leading to the recreation room in the paneled basement. Above the stairs leading to the basement we installed an elegant chandelier, so that when one went down to the rec room

the impression was that of going into another highly re-
fined and sophisticated living area, not into the "kids'
room."

In four months the house sold. It impressed Jeane Dix-
on, the forecaster who is also a leading real estate agent in
Washington, and she quickly sold it to an Air Force general for $150,000. After deducting the rehabilitation costs
and the selling commission, our profit on the transaction
amounted to exactly $6,102.33. The income tax on this
profit was about 33 percent, leaving a net after-tax profit
of about $4,000, not a bad profit on a $35,000 investment
for four months.

Perhaps this profit should be subtracted from the total
net investment in our homes to this point. If so, the
$13,000 net investment should be reduced by $4,000,
making $9,000.

Home Number Seven

Now we turned our attention once again to very elegant homes, and one of these we found in Greenwich,
Connecticut. Although Greenwich has a large total land
area amounting to forty-eight square miles, one almost
never can find a bargain there. It is an elegant community with a prestigious reputation. An additional attraction
is that Greenwich is the nearest Connecticut town to
New York City, and Connecticut has no state income tax
whereas New York State most certainly has an income tax
which shows signs only of rising.

For many months we looked in Greenwich without
buying. Every house seemed too costly. Then, in the recession of 1970, we found what we felt suited us well. It
was a large red brick Colonial with pillars on the front
porch. It had sixteen rooms and five baths plus a powder
room. It also had a three-car built-in garage, a side porch,
and at the rear a large concrete terrace that overlooked
the terraced lawns, a swimming pool, and a pond. In all,
there were over two and a half acres of terraced land

with about a hundred mature trees, thirty-three of them in front of the house. The entire property was enclosed by a high stone wall. The landscaping was recent and had cost about $12,000.

As in the case of other houses we had purchased, the owners were anxious to sell. They had priced the house at $275,000 and had not been able to find a buyer for about a year. The husband had been transferred to Ohio but the family could not move there until the Greenwich house was sold, so the husband had to commute every weekend—not a pleasing arrangement.

We bought the house for $190,000, but a good deal of additional expenditure was necessary, and quickly. The tile roof had to be repaired. The grounds had to be cleaned up. Under the terrace was a dirt floor area piled with junk. After this was cleaned out, a cement floor was laid, ornamental lights were installed, and the area was painted white. It became a kind of party area with natural wood tables and benches.

Extensive painting and plastering had to be done. Old bath fixtures were replaced. Wall-to-wall carpeting—thousands of dollars' worth of it—was laid all over the house. Two dozen chandeliers were installed. Shutters were added to all the windows.

When we finished the renovation work the $210,000 we had secured from Home Number Four in Rye had been invested in the Greenwich house. Very quickly we rented this house, and the tenants required that other improvements be made, but almost all of these were expenditures that could be charged against the high rent.

Six years later this house has been put on the market, after having been rented for almost four years. The asking price is $340,000. The actual selling price is anyone's guess, but we have received an offer on it in excess of our investment in it. We still have $35,500 actual cash invested in it up the line from Home Number One, or about $9,000 if we consider the series of home purchases and sales as "real estate transactions" and the profits on Home Number Five in Westport and Home Number Six in Washington are subtracted from this total investment.

Even if we do not subtract these profits, $35,500 is not an excessive amount for any family to invest in a home or homes over a period of twenty years, as we did. Some of our investments were in cash; others in time payments. Thus, $35,500 spread over twenty years equals $1,775 a year, or $148 a month.

How tax deferral works

The significant thing about the special Internal Revenue Service treatment of transactions involving selling one's home and buying another is that under certain circumstances there is no tax on any gain on the home one sells. These are the possibilities:

You may find another home better suited to your needs and preferences before you sell your old home. If so, you can buy the new home, provided it costs at least as much as what you will get on the old one, up to eighteen months prior to the time you sell your old home, and defer any profit on the sale.

Alternatively, you can sell your old home. Then you know how much money you have to put into another home. If you put all the money into the new home, any tax on the profit on the old home is deferred indefinitely. You have eighteen months to look for a new home after you sell the old one.

Thus you can buy a new home within eighteen months before or within eighteen months after you sell your old home. If you do not buy a new home within this eighteen-month period either side of the selling date of your old house then you must pay a capital gains tax on any profit realized on the sale.

If you choose to build a new home rather than buy an existing house the rules are more liberal. You must complete it and occupy it within two years after selling your

old home. But the total time period allowed for construction and occupancy of the new house is forty-two months,
beginning eighteen months before and ending two years
after the sale of your old house.

The law applies only to one's principal residence, not to
a second home or a vacation home, but the term "home"
includes cooperative apartments and condominiums as
well as houses.

In order to determine whether there is a gain on the
sale of the old house it is necessary to add to its purchase
price the cost of any improvements and additions made
to the house, and there must be records of this work.

Fix-up expenses are those that have been incurred in
order to get the house in condition to sell. These are not
added to the cost of the house. Instead they are deducted
from the selling price. If you have invested $50,000 in
your old house, including a purchase price of $49,000 and
a porch added at a cost of $1,000, then this is your adjust-
ed basis. Let us suppose you then spend $1,000 to paint
the house so that it looks better to a prospective buyer.
Let us further suppose that you sell the house for
$52,000.* You must reinvest only $51,000, not $52,000, as
your $1,000 fix-up expenses are deducted in determining
what you actually received for the house. These expenses
for fixing up must have been incurred within ninety days
of the sale date of the house; otherwise they are not deductible from the selling price in order to determine how
much must be reinvested in another house for the purpose of deferring the tax.

In this hypothetical sale you made a $1,000 profit on
the old house. It was sold for $52,000, but the fix-up ex-
penses were $1,000, and $50,000 had been invested in its
purchase price and the new porch.

If you buy a new house for $51,000 you defer any tax
on the $1,000 gain. If you reinvest in a new house only

---

* Net price received after any sales commission, legal costs, etc.

Form **2119**	**Sale or Exchange of Personal Residence**	**Taxable year**

Form **2119**
(Rev. Nov. 1976)
Department of the Treasury
Internal Revenue Service

▶ **Attach to Form 1040.**

Note: *Do not include expenses which are deductible as moving expenses on Form 3903.*

Name(s) as shown on Form 1040 | Your social security number

1(a) Date former residence sold

(e) Were any rooms in either residence rented or used for business purposes at any time? . .   Yes No
(If "Yes," explain on separate sheet and attach.)

(b) Have you ever deferred any gain on the sale or exchange of a personal residence? . . . .   Yes No

(c) Have you ever claimed a credit for purchase or construction of a new principal residence?
(If you answered "Yes," see Form 5405, Part II.)

(f) If you were married, do you and your spouse have the same proportionate ownership interest in your new residence as you had in your old residence? . . . .
(If "No," see the Consent on other side.)

2(a) Date new residence bought

3(a) Were you 65 or older on date of sale? . . . .
(If you answered "Yes," see Note below.)

(b) If new residence was constructed for or by you, date construction began

(c) Date you occupied new residence

(b) If you answered "Yes" to 3(a), did you use the property sold as your principal residence for a total of at least 5 years (except for short temporary absences) of the 8-year period preceding the sale? . . . .

(d) Were both the old and new properties used as your principal residence? . . . . . .   Yes No

(c) If you answered "Yes" to 3(b), do you want to elect to exclude gain on the sale from your gross income? . . .

Computation of Gain and Adjusted Sales Price

4 Selling price of residence. (Do not include selling price of personal property items.)	4	
5 Less: Commissions and other expenses of sale (from Schedule I on other side)	5	
6 Amount realized	6	
7 Less: Basis of residence sold (from Schedule II on other side)	7	
8 Gain on sale (line 6 less line 7). If line 7 is more than line 6, there is no gain, so you should not make further entries on this form	8	
9 Fixing-up expenses (from Schedule III on other side)	9	
10 Adjusted sales price (line 6 less line 9)	10	

If you answered "No" to question 3(a) or 3(c), complete only lines 11 through 14.
If you answered "Yes" to question 3(c), complete lines 15 through 17, or 15 through 20, whichever is applicable.

Computation of Gain to be Reported and Adjusted Basis of New Residence—General Rule

11 Cost of new residence	11	
12 Gain taxable this year (line 10 less line 11, but not more than line 8). If line 11 is more than line 10, enter zero. Enter here and on Schedule D (Form 1040), in column f, line 1, or line 6, whichever is applicable	12	
13 Gain on which tax is to be deferred (line 8 less line 12)	13	
14 Adjusted basis of new residence (line 11 less line 13)	14	

Computation of Exclusion, Gain to be Reported, and Adjusted Basis of New Residence—Special Rule
(For use of taxpayers 65 years of age or over who checked "Yes," in 3(c) above.)

15 If line 10 above is $20,000 or less, the entire gain shown on line 8 is excludable from gross income. If line 10 is over $20,000, determine the excludable portion of the gain as follows:		
(a) Divide amount on line 10 into $20,000 . . . . 15(a)		
(b) Excludable portion of gain (multiply amount on line 8 by figure on line 15(a) and enter result here) .	15(b)	
16 Nonexcludable portion of gain (line 8 less line 15(b))	16	
17 Cost of new residence. If a new personal residence was not purchased, enter "None," and do not complete the following lines. Then enter the amount shown on line 16 on Schedule D (Form 1040), in column f, line 6	17	
18 Gain taxable this year. (Line 10 less sum of lines 15(b) and 17. But this amount may not exceed line 16.) If line 17 plus line 15(b) is more than line 10, enter zero. Enter here and on Schedule D (Form 1040), in column f, line 6	18	
19 Gain on which tax is to be deferred (line 16 less line 18)	19	
20 Adjusted basis of new residence (line 17 less line 19)	20	

Note: There is a special provision available if you were 65 or older on the date of the sale or exchange of your principal residence. If you met the age requirement and owned and used the residence disposed of as your principal residence for a total of 5 years out of the 8 years preceding the sale, you may elect to exclude part or all of the gain from that sale. If the property is held by you and your spouse as joint tenants, tenants by the entirety, or community property and you and your spouse file joint return, only you or your spouse need meet the age requirement. You are only eligible for the exclusion once. This is true regardless of your marital status at the time you made the election.

Consent of You and Your Spouse to Apply Separate Gain on Sale of Old Residence to Basis of New Residence

Note: *The following Consent need not be completed if there was no gain on the sale of the old residence. If, however, there was a gain, and if the ownership interests of you and your spouse in the old and new residences were not in the same proportion, the separate gain on the sale of the old residence will be separately taxable to you and your spouse unless this Consent is filed.*

	Your portion	Spouse's portion
Adjusted sales price of old residence (from line 10)	$	$
Cost of new residence (from line 11 or 17)	$	$

The undersigned taxpayers, you and your spouse, consent to have the basis of the joint or separate interest in the new residence reduced by the amount of the joint or separate gain on the sale of the old residence which is not taxable solely by reason of the filing of this Consent.

Your signature	Date
Spouse's signature	Date

SCHEDULE I—Commissions and Other Expenses of Sale (Line 5)

This includes sales commissions, advertising expenses, attorney and legal fees, etc., incurred to effect the sale of the old residence. Enter the name and address of the payee and the date of payment for each item.

Item explanation	Amount
	$

SCHEDULE II—Basis of Old Residence (Line 7)

This includes the original cost of the property to the taxpayer, commissions, and other expenses incurred in its purchase, the cost of improvements, etc., less the total of the depreciation allowed or allowable (if any), all casualty losses previously allowed (if any), and the nontaxable gain (if any) on the sale or exchange of a previous personal residence.

Item explanation	Amount
	$

SCHEDULE III—Fixing-up Expenses (Line 9)

These are decorating and repair expenses which were incurred solely to assist in the sale of the old property, and which are not ordinarily deductible in computing taxable income nor taken into account in computing the basis of the old residence or the amount realized from its sale. Fixing-up expenses must have been incurred for work performed within 90 days before the contract to sell was signed, and must have been paid for not later than 30 days after the sale.

Item explanation	Date work performed	Date paid	Amount
			$

For more information obtain Publication 523, Tax Information on Selling or Purchasing Your Home, from your local IRS office.

the $50,000 you had in the old house, your capital gain is $1,000, and on this you must pay the capital gains tax. If you buy a house for $50,500 you must pay a capital gains tax on $500. If your new house costs $48,000 you would still be obligated to pay a tax on only $1,000, which is the profit you made on the sale of your old house. This is because you pay the tax on your profit from the sale of your old house *or* the difference between the adjusted sales price of the old house and the purchase price of the new house, *whichever is less.*

It is possible to "step down" in this way. You may have bought a series of houses, making a profit on each but reinvesting all of the proceeds of your previous houses. You may thus buy a $200,000 house at the end of a series of sales and purchases but have only $50,000 invested in the $200,000 house. Now you may want to get some of your capital out of that house. When you sell it for, say, $225,000, you may want to buy another house for only $175,000. Because you have deferred paying the capital gains tax on your previous home sales, the difference between the adjusted sales price of the old house and the purchase price of the new house will be less than your profit from the sale of your old house. You will therefore pay a capital gains tax on the difference between $225,000, the sales price of the old house, and the $175,000 purchase price of the new house. Your capital gain subject to the tax is thus $50,000.

If you sell your principal residence at age sixty-five or older and have occupied it for at least five of the eight years preceding the sale, you may not have to pay a capital gains tax if you choose not to buy another house. The price at which you sell the house must be no more than $35,000 if the entire capital gains tax is to be eliminated. If the house sells for more than $35,000, as many houses today do, tax is payable at increasing percentages of the capital gain.

Internal Revenue Service Publication 523, titled *Tax*

A HOME AS AN INVESTMENT

Information on Selling Your Home, goes into the tax-deferral provisions in detail. The same information is contained in *Your Federal Income Tax,* issued by the Internal Revenue Service and revised each year.

For a capital gain on a home of $50,000 or less, the capital gains tax is 25 percent. Alternatively, one can include as ordinary income one-half of the capital gain, and this may result in a smaller tax than 25 percent on the gain of under $50,000, or 35 percent of the gain if more than $50,000.

Buying a home with investment value

A home and life insurance are the major assets of a large percentage of Americans. Very often a person has a great deal of money invested in a life insurance policy and a home, and these investments have generally been made by installment payments over a period of years. Such payments are a kind of periodic saving that increased the cash value of the policy and wholly or partially paid off the mortgage on the house. Many people with sizable investments in life insurance policies and homes have little else in the way of capital.

Since one of the two major assets of many people is a house, the house should be selected most carefully, far more carefully than a portfolio of securities which can be sold quickly if they do not perform as expected. If you make a mistake in investing in a house it is much harder to divest yourself of the mistake. It takes time to find a buyer and to get the "right price." In fact the right price may not be obtained at all. Thus, it is important to choose well when buying a house.

Your house is first of all a home—the place in which you live, where your family lives, the place from which you go to work and to which you return at night. It is the place where you entertain friends. It is an integral part of your life. For these reasons we might view a house in relation to what it is supposed to do and be:

1. *A dwelling convenient to the breadwinner's place of business.* Location is of chief importance in selecting a home.

2. *A dwelling suitable to the family.* If there are three children in the family, it may be desirable to have a home with four bedrooms. If the home is to be occupied by a childless couple, two bedrooms may be the maximum number required.

3. *A good investment.* The primary requirements to be filled by a home are to provide adequate shelter for the family and to be convenient to the breadwinner's place of work. After these requirements have been met, investment value should be considered. This is the aspect we will emphasize, but not forgetting the preceding two requirements.

The chief investment criteria for the home buyer to consider are these:

• The house should be likely to rise in value. This can be judged by the present value and "growth potential" of other properties in the same area or in other areas in which the buyer may have an interest.

• If possible, the house should be purchased under the market price. Too few investors realize that one of the objectives or "tricks" of investing is to "buy right." If a wise purchase price is arrived at, then the job of selling in the future is made far easier.

• When the house that has been bought is offered for sale at some time in the future, the owner should price it under the market in the area. It is possible to do this if the house was bought well, which usually means bought under the market. In any event, whether it was bought well or not, pricing under the market sells a house much faster than pricing at or above the market. Sometimes houses priced "right" will sell on the same day they are placed on the market.

First consider the area

This is a period of rapid change. Areas are not changing slowly as they did before World War II and in the first fifteen years of the postwar era. The entire Southwest is growing by leaps and bounds and property values have been rising steadily. New York City real estate has been in trouble for the past three years, during which time the Connecticut suburbs have been booming. Newark and Jersey City also are in trouble and many good houses have been abandoned by their owners. Overall there is a movement to the Southwest. There is also a movement out of the cities, and there is a movement out of the suburbs that have high taxes and high rates for utilities supplied by the metropolitan electric, gas, and water companies.

Within the cities themselves there have been massive population shifts—into certain areas and out of others, and the latter often become crime-ridden and experience declining home values.

It is important to get the present feel of an area and to form some idea as to which way it is moving. What will the area be like five years from now? Are new homes being built in it? What kinds of new homes—expensive or cheap ones? What is the zoning—quarter-acre, an acre, more than an acre? Is industry permitted? If so, is it light or heavy industry? Are stores allowed alongside homes or close to them?

Next consider the street

The way to determine the best streets and the best blocks of the best streets is to drive around a good deal with informed real estate agents. Only then can you form a judgment as to the best residential locations in a town or general area.

In one block on Wyoming Avenue just off Connecticut Avenue in Washington, D.C., there are two embassies of foreign governments as well as other official residences

Fast-Growing Cities

Among the nation's 100 largest cities these grew most rapidly between 1970 and 1975:

	1975 Population	Increase Since 1970
1. Huntington Beach, Calif.	149,706	29.1%
2. Colorado Springs, Colo.	179,584	27.8%
3. Anchorage, Alaska	161,018	27.4%
4. Virginia Beach, Va.	213,954	24.3%
5. San Jose, Calif.	555,707	20.5%
6. El Paso, Tex.	385,691	19.7%
7. Austin, Tex.	301,147	17.7%
8. Anaheim, Calif.	193,616	16.4%
9. Las Vegas, Nev.	146,030	16.1%
10. Albuquerque, N.M.	279,401	14.6%

Shrinking Cities

Among the nation's 100 largest cities these lost population most rapidly between 1970 and 1975:

	1975 Population	Decrease Since 1970
1. Dayton, Ohio	205,986	−15.8%
2. Saint Louis, Mo.	524,964	−15.6%
3. Cleveland, Ohio	638,793	−14.9%
4. Minneapolis, Minn.	378,112	−13.0%
5. Buffalo, N.Y.	407,160	−12.0%
6. Atlanta, Ga.	436,057	−11.9%
7. Detroit, Mich.	1,335,085	−11.8%
8. Pittsburgh, Pa.	458,651	−11.8%
9. Newark, N.J.	339,568	−11.1%
10. Gary, Ind.	167,546	−11.1%

Source: U.S. Bureau of the Census

and several extremely fine private homes worth well into
six figures. Just around a corner is one of the finest and
most expensive houses in Washington, worth over
$500,000 and proposed as the official residence of the
chief justice of the United States Supreme Court. However, just two blocks away, on the other side of Connecticut
Avenue but still on Wyoming Avenue, is one of the most
violent streets in the entire city, a block characterized by
break-ins and muggings. Only when the residents hired
their own armed patrol and illuminated every house on
the street did the crime subside.

Here is another example of the importance of the
street on which a house is situated: So popular is exclusive
Round Hill Road in Greenwich, Connecticut, that prospective house purchasers often state that they are interested only in houses located on Round Hill Road, even
though some of them have never even seen Round Hill
Road!

Then consider the house

These are the aspects of a house that a prospective buyer might consider:

The architecture. The architectural style of the house
should be of a type popular and valuable in the area. A
Georgian Colonial is very much wanted in Southport,
Connecticut. It is not so much wanted in Scottsdale, Arizona. The popular style in Arizona is the ranch house on
one level. Mediterranean styles are popular in California.
They are much less popular in Connecticut. In fact in
many areas in the East the Mediterranean styles are not
in demand, and one might note that the mortgage departments of banks and savings and loan associations in
the East are often not much in favor of Mediterraneans as
collateral.

In the eastern United States the Tudor style seems to
be increasing in popularity. The gables, wood exterior
beams, beamed ceilings, and mullioned windows of this

style are by no means 100 percent accepted today, although they certainly were in the East in the 1920s.

The Elizabethan house is more preferred in the East.
In this style the exterior has more brick and less white
plaster than in the Tudor style. The curved arch is used in
the Elizabethan as in the Tudor but exterior wood is less
used.

The "no-style" house of the 1920s and early 1930s is
not in particular demand, although demand seems to be
growing in the East even for this type of house.

Early in the postwar era the ultramodern "abstract"
house of super-efficient design appeared to be the house
of the future, but the style did not catch on as well as had
been forecast. Some of these "houses of the future" sell
for quite low prices, particularly in the East, after having
been on the market for some time.

The size. This is the most important element of the
house after the style of architecture. Fifteen years ago
very large houses, often palatial homes of a bygone era,
were known as white elephants. They were often sold for
whatever they would bring after the estates of which
they were the dwellings were divided and sold.

Ten years ago the label of white elephant began to disappear, and large, particularly large and palatial, houses
rose sharply in both prestige and price, along with Rolls-
Royce cars, yachts, and old master paintings.

Then with the advent of high prices for fuel oil a trend
started away from the largest houses to smaller but still
elegant houses, and particularly to those with low heating
bills, low utilities bills, and low maintenance costs for
house and grounds. It is this size of house that has recently experienced the largest price increase.

The in-demand smaller house should still have a large
number of bedrooms plus a recreation room, a dining
room, a breakfast room or alcove, a library, a powder
room, a bar with running water and a refrigerator, and a
terrace. A newly wanted feature is a wine cellar, prefer-

ably an air-conditioned one to keep the wine at a constant temperature of fifty-five to sixty degrees.

A swimming pool is an attraction and value element, particularly if it is heated. Ranking after a pool as wanted features are a tennis court and, in newer houses, a sauna.

The equipment. First in importance when checking the equipment of a house is the plumbing system. It should be in good condition and preferably of recent origin or at least recently overhauled completely. If the pipes are copper, that is certainly a plus.

Next comes the heating system. Is the furnace modern? It is a value-adding feature if the house has a five-zone hot-water one-pipe baseboard heating system of recent origin.

A radiator system is less desirable than a baseboard system. Vapor-vacuum is less desirable than hot water, and steam is even less desirable. The old type of hot-air system is virtually an immediate candidate for a costly replacement. Modern electric hot-air systems must be studied individually. They can either be great pluses or candidates for replacement, depending on the system.

Circulating hot water is a highly desirable feature, although some modern houses do not have such a system. If the water is not circulated by a motor it takes time for the taps to run hot water, and water is wasted while waiting for it to become hot.

The wiring system is very important. An old system in a large house can cost a fortune to repair. This writer recently spent about $12,000 to put in a modern wiring system in a large house abroad. Had the same work been done in this country, the wiring system could well have cost four times that figure.

If the wiring is enclosed in plastic or other tubes in the wall, it is a distinct plus for the house. There should be circuit-breakers of modern design. If the house has 220 volts running into it in addition to the 110-volt system this is a value-adding feature. What is the capacity of the electric system of the house? Can it handle all appliances plus perhaps a central air-conditioning system? Even in areas where temperatures are moderate, an air-conditioning system, centrally installed, adds value. In some areas a house is difficult to sell if it lacks a modern central air-conditioning system.

A modern kitchen can easily cost $10,000, and most homeowners want modern kitchens. It therefore may be surprising that this element does not appear earlier on our list of home-value determinants, but the condition of the kitchen does not seem very important to most home buyers. They apparently feel able to install kitchens to suit their personal preferences after buying their homes.

An adequate bathroom can cost as little as $2,000. If luxurious equipment is wanted, the cost can rise to as much as for a kitchen. If the house has superior bath equipment this is very much of a plus. Most homeowners think several times before installing faucets at $500 a pair, but such an installation says a great deal to a prospective buyer about the owner's investment in the house and its upkeep.

Burglar-alarm systems and systems to detect fire and smoke are increasingly becoming necessities. If the present rate of housebreaking continues, a burglar-alarm system may be an absolute must ten years from now. A burglar-alarm system adds at least its cost to the value of any house.

The condition. Price is often determined or modified by a house's condition. Our house on Wyoming Avenue in Washington, referred to earlier in this chapter as Home Number Two, was priced at $38,000. When a tour of the house revealed its poor condition the real estate agent was persuaded that $28,000 was a reasonable offer, and this offer was finally accepted by the owner. Very often poor condition is mentioned to prospective buyers by the real estate agent with the implication that a low offer might be acceptable to the owner.

On the other hand, a superbly maintained house is praised by the real estate agent before it is even shown, the implication being that one should feel lucky to get such a fine house for such a reasonable asking price. Actually, mint condition means a disproportionately high price in many cases, while poor condition results in a price that may be disproportionately low.

These elements of condition should be checked:

The wood should be examined. The main danger is termites, and the owner should provide a guarantee against termites or a certificate from a qualified termite-inspection firm. In addition, the wood should not be rotten because of a lack of surface covering, mainly paint. Floors under carpets should be inspected for rot and excessive wear. Various worms and beetles can literally destroy a house.

The roof should be carefully inspected by a qualified roofer. The heavy slate roof of our Home Number Three, mentioned earlier, would have cost $50,000 to replace. Actually, one year this roof and another one shared the roofers' prize for the finest roofs in America.

Bricks and masonry should be checked very carefully in every part of the house. Bricks and cement are easy to replace, but it is possible that broken bricks and mortar have admitted water over a period of time so that wood under the bricks has rotted—a situation that can cost a fortune to rectify.

Gutters and drains should be examined. These may have to be extensively replaced. If they are of lead or copper it is a big plus, as either type is costly but lasts virtually forever.

The exterior water and drainage systems should be good. Check the history of the drainage system, including any septic tank. A new septic tank and lines can save large expenses later. The water lines of the house should be in good repair and of recent origin. A plan of the water lines and tanks should be made available to the home buyer, as stoppages are hard to locate without knowing where the pipes and tanks are.

Cellar leaks should be noted. Many houses have cellars that leak and accumulate water on the floor. This is a very difficult problem to solve and may entail digging and repairing foundations far below the surface.

For a large house the cost of repainting the interior can run to $5,000 and even more. For this reason recent interior paint is a big asset. It adds to the appearance of the house and lasts for many years since it is not subject to wear by the elements.

Exterior paint must be applied every five years or even more often, so poor exterior paint is not as serious as poor interior paint. Even if the exterior paint is good, in a few years a new coat will have to be applied. An exterior paint job on a medium-sized house can cost $3,000 or more.

Consider the land and setting

A fact that seems to be frequently ignored by real estate agents is the value of the land on which a house is situated. It would seem that a house on one acre should be worth less than if it were on an acre and a half. Yet the importance of the amount of land with a house too often is overlooked. It may therefore be a good idea to pay particular attention to houses with more than the usual acreage as these can often be bought at prices that do not reflect the increased amount of land. The value of an acre or a half-acre of land is quite well known in every area, certainly by the real estate agents, and this value should be learned by the prospective house buyer. Of course there may not be enough additional land to sell off some. Nevertheless, the more land with the house the more valuable the house, as a general rule.

The location of the land and the placement of the house on it are important value-giving elements. If the house is on high land, particularly if it has a view, it is better than a house in a hollow, against a hill, or next to another house, with little or no view.

Is the land "as is" or is it landscaped? If landscaped, to what extent? Is it terraced? Terracing costs a good deal of money but adds greatly to the value of the land and thus the house. And landscaping can be expensive. In some cases the landscape architect or landscape gardener who did the work can be located in order to find out what the job cost. Then one can estimate what one would have had to spend had the landscaping not already been done.

Most important as a feature of the land and setting is the presence of water. If the house is a waterfront property, particularly if it is directly on the waterfront, its value is increased considerably. If the house is not on open water, it may be on a river—the next best location—or on a stream, a lake, or a pond. All of these bodies of water are value-adding features.

Check the neighborhood facilities

Under a general heading of facilities the most important consideration by far is the school system. This is true whether or not the buyer has children. The resale value of any house depends, in large measure, on the quality of the schools. In the 1960s poor schools developed as never before, and the good public school is now almost a rarity. It is possible that a good school system nearby can raise the value of a house by as much as 50 percent.

A large and effective police department is an important element in determining where to buy a house as well as in determining property values. Housebreakings and muggings are becoming more prevalent. The number of policemen on foot in a particular area and the number of patrol cars operating during the day and the night to a great degree affect the value of houses in any area.

Next in importance might be the fire department. If the fire department is large and well-equipped, and if

there are hydrants near the house, the value of the property is affected positively. Professional fire departments
are to be preferred over volunteer ones as a rule.

Nearness to a shopping area is important, and the
house-hunter should find out if the stores are of the quality and in the price range the family prefers.

Transportation facilities must be determined. Nearness
to a bus line is a plus. Many suburbs are linked to the city
by rail, and generally this service is rather poor and costly. Still it must be used by most commuters. Commuting
time to the city and nearness of the house to the suburban railroad station are factors of great importance.

If the rail line is old, as most are, the area is less desirable than if there is a local rail transportation authority or
Amtrak service. Reliability of the service is becoming almost as important as time to and from the city.

Taxi service can be of strategic importance, particularly for the commuter who uses it daily to travel between
home and the train station. Some taxi services are very
high in price; some are still relatively inexpensive.

Closely allied to bus and rail service is connecting service to airlines. If a town is a stop on a regular and frequent airline limousine service, that factor increases the
value of houses in the area. The nearness of the town to
the airport also is important. Some suburban communities are two hours from the airport by limousine, and the
limousine can then cost a good deal more than the now
"reasonable" $10 one-way fare.

Garage service is very much a part of the transportation picture for suburban communities and city neighborhoods. First of all, garage service should be adequate for
most common makes of cars. Second, it should not cost a
great deal, although $20 an hour is not an unusual repair
shop charge at the present time.

Are a plumber, an electrician, a carpenter, and a painter available in the area, or must they come from the city
or from a town ten miles away? Their per-hour charge is

now almost secondary to their availability, and in many areas $15 an hour is standard or even low.

Check on property taxes

The present level of taxes can be a very influential factor in deciding to buy a particular house and what price to pay for it. Our Home Number Three, in Bronxville, was priced at $195,000 fifteen years ago. The taxes were an extremely high $5,800 at the time. Because the house was very large and the taxes very high a sales impasse was created. The house finally sold for $65,000.

The trend of taxes is also important. One should find out what the property taxes were for several previous years. The trend to date may well be projected into the future at the same rate, or even at an accelerated rate. High taxes decrease the value of houses and low taxes raise their value.

For projections of taxes one might check the town records and determine assessed values as related to true values. Almost all communities tax at some percentage of true values. The Bronxville house referred to above, in Westchester County, New York, was assessed at $83,000, which was 55 percent of its true value of about $150,000—not very far from the asking price of $195,000. Still the house sold for $65,000.

One might also check the debt of the community in which the house being considered is located. A growing debt structure certainly indicates higher taxes in the future. No debt or limited debt mean taxes are unlikely to rise, which adds value to the house now as well as in the future.

The tax level in relation to nearby areas should be carefully studied. Taxes in Westchester County, New York, may be twice the level of those in adjoining Fairfield County, Connecticut. This situation means that home values in Westchester County are almost certainly well under those of Fairfield County, since it is easy to buy in

How the Property Tax Burden
Has Steadily Increased

Local property taxes increased 167 percent in the period 1960-75. The projection for 1980 assumes that the 11 percent average annual increase will continue.

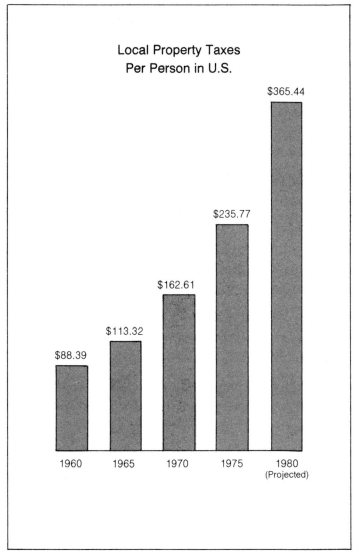

Local Property Taxes
Per Person in U.S.

$365.44

$235.77

$162.61

$113.32

$88.39

1960   1965   1970   1975   1980
                              (Projected)

Source: U.S. Bureau of the Census

Greenwich, Connecticut, instead of in Rye, New York, just five minutes away by car.

When the prospective home buyer reaches this point, taxes can be added to the heating bill, the electric bill, the water bill, the cost of grounds maintenance (and possibly pool maintenance), and the cost of repairs over a period of one year or more. It is unnecessary to proceed past this point if it is obvious that the total costs are too high for the buyer or too high to permit the buyer to sell the house in the future at a reasonable price.

Decor as a factor

Decoration is critical to a house's value. If the decoration is poor it usually does not cost much to make it good. The effect is far out of proportion to cost. Still, a poorly decorated house is shunned by real estate agents. Also, if the curtains and the furniture are not attractive, an agent is not inclined to push the house—unimportant though curtains and furniture may seem to the buyer who wants a house, not furnishings.

Agents seem to go out of their way to say, "Now you will have to overlook the poor decor. You can change that easily enough." At this juncture many buyers will disagree and walk out of the house quickly. On the other hand, a well-decorated house tends to make a potential buyer "fall in love with it." Decoration can quickly eliminate a house from a potential buyer's consideration or quickly clinch the deal.

The house is a package which should appeal to the new owners in addition to satisfying their technical requirements for a dwelling suitable to their needs that is also a potential money-maker.

The knowledgeable person buys a house that looks terrible but requires very little expenditure to make it look attractive. Such a person wants to buy a structurally sound and well-designed house that sells under the market because it does not have mass appeal, and that can with minimum expense become an attractive home plus a money-maker in the not too distant future.

Renting your home

Apart from its resale value, a home can be a good business proposition. The home can be rented when the owner goes on a vacation abroad or accepts a temporary business assignment in another part of the country or another part of the world. Such an arrangement also can be used as a temporary expedient if the owner moves away but cannot for a time find a buyer for the house.

To indicate the possible profit in renting one's residence, let us take as an example the rental of our Home Number Four in Rye, New York, for one summer. The house was not advertised as a rental. The real estate agent who had sold us the house simply said that he had a client who wanted to rent a waterfront property for the summer and then asked us whether we were interested.

We were interested, particularly at the proposed rent— $1,000 per week for almost nine weeks—$8,800 in all.

We accepted the offer, made reservations for Europe for the summer, and worked out our profit-and-loss forecast, which turned out to be our actual profit and loss:

Rental income for the summer		$8,800.00
Less rental commission		880.00
Net rental income		7,920.00
Less repairs—for children's safety		1,990.16
		5,929.84
Less prorated property taxes		954.00
		4,975.84
Less prorated insurance		54.00
		4,921.84
Less depreciation:		
Dwelling	$1,111.00	
Furniture	345.80	1,456.80
Net profit		$3,465.04

It can, of course, be argued that the taxes and insurance would have to be paid anyway and therefore should not be deducted. In any event taxes for the year are a deduction on one's personal income tax Form 1040, as are interest expenses. In the case of this house there was no mortgage, thus no deductible interest expense.

Depreciation would also continue anyway; but depreciation is often the key to a profitable home rental. With depreciation, the rental may well be profitable; without it, the rental may not be profitable at all.

Depreciaton is in one sense the decline in the value of an asset with time. A car wears out over a period of time. So do a house and home furnishings. In another sense, depreciation is a putting aside of cash for the purpose of eventually replacing an old asset with a new one. Such cash, in accounting, is set aside in a reserve for depreciation.

Depreciation as a key element

When you rent out your residence it is considered "used" housing for depreciation purposes. If a $40,000 house, for example, still has a useful life of at least twenty years, $2,000 can be charged for depreciation each year over the twenty years, making $40,000 charged for depreciation during the life of the house. This is the "straight-line" method of depreciation, in which the same amount is taken for depreciation each year.

There is also accelerated depreciation, which allows a property to be depreciated faster in the early years of its rental. For used residential rental property the 125 percent declining balance method is the most rapid depreciation permitted. However, if such a property has less than a twenty-year life remaining it must be depreciated under the straight-line method.

Under the 125 percent depreciation method, if a house cost $40,000 and can be depreciated for twenty years, then $2,500 can be the depreciation for the first year.

This figure is subtracted from the $40,000 cost, and next year there is only $37,500 to depreciate. In this way the depreciation charge declines each year. There cannot be a complete depreciation; there must be some "salvage value" left at the end of the depreciation process.

The usual basis for depreciation is the price you paid to purchase the property—minus the value of the land—plus the costs of permanent improvements you have made on the house.

As far as furnishings are concerned, it is possible that the Internal Revenue Service will accept a useful life of six years, although to be accurate these assets should be classified and depreciated by groups—curtains, carpets, furniture, and so forth.

If the furnishings have a useful life of at least three years, then the 150 percent declining balance method may be used.

If there are $12,000 worth of used furnishings in the $40,000 house, then one-sixth of the furnishings' cost—$2,000—may be charged off each year under the straight-line method. If the 150 percent method is used, $3,000 can be charged as depreciation for the furniture and fixtures for the first year. This sum is subtracted from the $12,000 total cost of the furnishings and the balance is depreciated by the 150 percent declining-balance method the following year—and so on, until the depreciation charge diminishes to nothing.

The depreciation on the $40,000 property containing furnishings worth $12,000 can be for the first year $2,500 on the house plus $3,000 on the furnishings, making $5,500 in all.

On a $200,000 house with $30,000 worth of used furnishings, the depreciation for the first year can be $12,500 for the house, and $7,500 for the furnishings—a total of $20,000.

There is one other major depreciation provision, and this is called the "Additional First-Year Depreciation" by the Internal Revenue Service, which says: "If you acquire personal property for use in your business or for the production of income, you may be entitled, in the first year, to deduct 20 percent of the cost of the property in addition to your regular depreciation. You do not use salvage value in computing this deduction. The additional depreciation is figured before you determine your regular depreciation deduction.

"Qualifying property is tangible personal property, such as office furniture, having a useful life of at least six years from the date you acquire it. The property may be new or used."

The limit on the cost of total personal property on which the special depreciation is allowed is $10,000 for those filing separate tax returns or $20,000 for husband and wife filing a joint return. Twenty percent of $20,000 is $4,000, the maximum first-year depreciation that those filing joint returns can claim.

To the $20,000 depreciation in our hypothetical $200,000 rental house, this $4,000 can be added, making a total of $24,000.

If, to this sum, taxes of, say, $4,500 a year and interest of 8 percent on a $100,000 mortgage—$8,000—are added, for a total of $36,500, it is not difficult to see that the rented house is not likely to show a profit. A rental of over $2,000 a month, or $24,000 a year, for a furnished $200,000 house is the great exception, and a red figure appears on the bottom line for this rental property.

Of course, the rental commission to the real estate agent, house repairs, and insurance must be added to the expenses. Still, these expenses (with the exception of the rental commission) and payments for mortgage interest and insurance would continue even if the house were not rented. Thus, how much one makes or loses on a rental depends to a considerable extent on theory, particularly depreciation theory—as promulgated by the Internal Revenue Service.

Examples of income from rentals

Our first rental, of Home Number One in Washington, D.C., was to a business establishment. In this case accelerated depreciation was not used and the $17,500 house was depreciated over a forty-year period. Depreciation worked out to $438 a year. Interest on the mortgage at 5 percent per year amounted to $600 annually. Taxes were a remarkably low $120 a year and insurance was about $300. Repairs were undertaken by the tenant, who also paid the utility and heating bills. The rental was $450 per month—$5,400 a year. All of the expenses to be borne by us amounted to $1,458 a year. Our new income was thus $3,942.

The return on our $17,500 purchase price was 22½ percent a year. On the actual cash invested of $5,500, the return was about 70 percent a year.

To illustrate how accelerated depreciation reduces tax liability, we can take the case of our Home Number Seven in Greenwich, Connecticut, which cost $190,000 plus about $20,000 in rehabilitation.

This is a statement of the income and expenses on the property for the first year it was rented:

Rental for 12 months		$24,000.00
Insurance	$1,565.00	
Repairs	1,757.85	
Rental commission	1,800.00	
Moving furniture out	3,222.44	
Property tax	3,502.35	
Yard and pool maintenance	953.50	
Depreciation	21,830.49	
Total	$34,631.63	34,631.63
Loss		$10,631.63

The depreciation on $32,572 worth of furniture at a rate of 150 percent declining balance over six years, plus $4,000 first-year depreciation, plus the depreciation on the house valued at $155,000 depreciated at a rate of 125 percent declining balance results in a total depreciation of $21,830.49.

Were it not for this depreciation, the loss of $10,631.63 would be turned into a profit of $11,198.86, not a very good return on a $210,000 house plus $32,572 worth of furnishings—$242,572 invested in cash and with no mortgage. The big plus here is the depreciation which results in a red bottom-line figure (loss) of $10,631.63.

This means that if our other income amounted to just this figure—$10,631.63—we would pay no income tax at all. If our income were around $45,000 to $65,000—in the approximately 50 percent tax bracket—this $10,631.63 red figure would save us half of this amount in taxes by reducing our income by this sum.

To a person with a $200,000 income from investments, the $10,631.63 would be worth 70 percent in tax savings—$7,442.

While the homeowner is securing tax advantages and income from the rented residence, the property is likely to be appreciating in value. The home thus provides a periodic return and if chosen well should also be an equity that can be sold for a capital gain without any tax liability, provided the proceeds are reinvested in another home. A home may therefore prove to be the best possible investment for a wealth-builder.

6

Investing
in
Collectibles

The number of people who have acquired a sizable fund of wealth through collectibles has increased tremendously in the period since 1950. In the early 1970s, in particular, many people realized large sums of money either on individual items they owned or on collections they built up during recent years.

The sale at Christie's in London on June 24-25, 1974, of the Frederick M. Mayer collection may well rank as the most amazing sale of a collection in history. The amazing aspect is the selling prices of the items in relation to their costs a relatively short time prior to the auction.

Frederick Mayer came to New York from Vienna in 1937 and went into the real estate and stock brokerage business. In 1945 he began collecting Chinese objects. Most of his collecting was apparently done during a peri-

How Antique Chinese Ceramics
Have Soared in Value

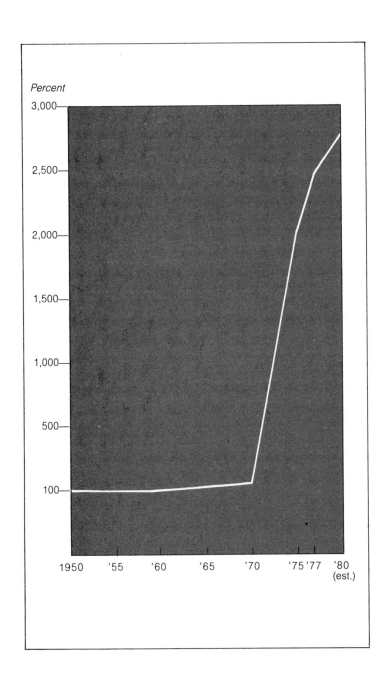

od of fifteen years. A total of 228 items from his collection, principally Chinese ceramics, were sold during the two-day auction.

One item was a Northern celadon shallow globular incense burner on three molded lions' mask and paw feet. It was 7⅛ inches high and the diameter at the lip was 8½ inches. This piece was purchased in London in the 1950s for 28 pounds—at that time about $100. In the 1974 sale a Chinese buyer purchased it for 99,750 pounds sterling—$239,400.

Another item was a blue and white pear-shaped ewer, 13¼ inches high. It was bought at auction in London in the 1950s for 90 pounds. At the 1974 sale it brought 73,500 pounds—$176,400.

The star of the sale was a fourteenth-century blue and white baluster jar (Mei P'ing). It was of octagonal shape, 17½ inches high, and featured paintings of a praying mantis, a female phoenix, a male phoenix, and a cockroach sitting on a grapevine.

Perry Rathbone, former director of Boston's Museum of Fine Arts and later director of Christie's in New York, recalls that Mr. Mayer was interested in purchasing the jar at an auction in Cologne, Germany, in 1948 but was unable to attend the sale. He persuaded a friend to bid on the piece for him. The friend was successful at the auction and purchased the jar for the equivalent of $800. On June 24, 1974, the jar sold for 220,000 pounds—$554,400.

The total realized at the Mayer sale was 2,673,027 pounds sterling, or $6,415,265.

In the Headley Museum in Lexington, Kentucky, there is a smaller but distinguished collection of Chinese ceramics. It was put together by a couple who lived after World War II in Darien, Connecticut. They looked for Chinese objects in the New England area, and they were successful in their search.

When they placed their collection in the museum valuations were placed on the various pieces. Many of the items are valued in the high thousands of dollars and some of these pieces were purchased at prices around the $50 mark.

Among those who have also profited in this manner are Mr. and Mrs. Dino D'Angelo. In 1974 they brought an "object" to the Sotheby Parke Bernet clinic, which that firm held in Chicago to help people learn the value of the things they owned and at the same time to obtain some valuable pieces for the firm to auction.

The piece that the D'Angelos brought in was a T'ang dynasty pottery figure of a horse and a rider with a greyhound sitting on the lap of the rider. The D'Angelos had bought it in 1959 for under $3,000—about market price at that time—and wanted to know what it was worth in 1974.

Later that year Sotheby Parke Bernet auctioned the piece for the D'Angelos. It brought $92,500, an auction record price for any Chinese object sold in America up to that time.

This is the way Chinese ceramics rose in price in the postwar period. If one liked Chinese works of art and purchased them as a hobby or to decorate one's home, wealth-building would have resulted as a fringe benefit.

There were some unpredictable factors in the immense price rise of Chinese ceramics, of course. Prior to the governmental overturn in Portugal some of the wealthy families there fixed on Chinese ceramics as a good investment and, through London dealers, placed orders worth millions of dollars for such works of art. Thus, their assets could be transferred from Portugal by means of a prime collectible.

Another factor in the price rise was that the Japanese very much like Chinese ceramics. In the early 1970s the Japanese economy boomed and the yen rose in value. Many wealthy Japanese could hardly wait to buy such collectibles, and about 75 percent of the objects sold in the Mayer sale went to buyers from Japan.

How art has increased in value

Chinese ceramics are just one category of collectibles that have shown enormous appreciation in recent years. Particularly large increases have also occurred in the prices paid for various types of paintings, for example.

Many collectors hope to discover an artist who is unknown and who will one day, in the not-too-distant future, make it to the top. It is almost impossible to pick such a winner early enough to be able to collect the artist's works at reasonable prices. But this is not always the case. In 1974, Ruth Culberg Rosenberg of Chicago sold a Willem de Kooning abstract painting of a nude woman to the Australian National Gallery. Her first husband, the late Maurice Culberg, had bought the painting, *Woman V*, from the Sidney Janis Gallery in New York for $3,000 in 1953, one year after de Kooning painted it. To acquire this painting the Australian gallery paid Mrs. Culberg Rosenberg the sum of $850,000, which set a record for a painting by a living artist.

Then there was the experience of New York City taxicab owner Robert Scull who collected contemporary American art for thirteen years. He usually bought a painting when it was hot off the artist's easel. He sponsored new and what he considered to be innovative artists, and in the process became not only a pioneering art collector but a prominent person socially through his ownership of "mod" and "in" works of art. He also did all he could to promote the artists in whose work he was interested.

On the evening of October 18, 1973, Robert Scull sold fifty of his works of art in a tremendously publicized auction sale. The receipts from the sale totaled $2,242,900—for fifty items that had cost Mr. Scull about $130,000.

Just seven of the works—by Jasper Johns, Robert Rauschenberg, and Cy Twombly—sold for a total of $691,000. They had cost Mr. Scull $21,030. He received a gross of thirty-three times what he had paid for them.

To cite another example of the rise in art prices, an old master painting of flowers was purchased some years ago at a country auction for $1,500. When the painting was brought to Sotheby Parke Bernet to auction in December 1973 it was identified as being a rare work by French painter Louise Moillon. At the auction sale it was purchased for $120,000.

The most expensive painting ever sold at auction was the *Juan de Pareja* portrait by Velasquez. In 1970, Christie's secured for this painting the unprecedented price of 2,310,000 pounds, the equivalent of $5,544,000. It was bought by New York's Metropolitan Museum of Art, where it hangs today.

Lord Pleydell-Bouverie, a member of the family that sold the painting at auction, commented on the sale: "Of course this painting has been in our family a good number of years, but it is interesting to note the selling price in relation to what we originally paid for the painting, which was the equivalent of about $200."

Discoveries and the rising market

Such stories are a combination of two things: discoveries and the rapidly rising market for all collectibles. Discoveries are items purchased advantageously for one reason or another, or items whose real nature or identification is not known to the seller.

Consider these discoveries:

• A Venetian palace settee of green painted wood and gilt with a silk covering made by Scalamandré was purchased advantageously in the summer of 1970 at the Adam A. Weschler and Son auction house in Washington, D.C. The settee was large and a little elaborate for American homes. It was also sold fairly late in the evening of a big sale, and it happened to be a Saturday evening, when the New York dealers and the Washington retail buyers had for the most part completed their purchases and gone home. The settee sold for $225. The buyer immediately shipped it to Italy. There any dealer would pay ten times $225 for this piece, a great rarity in furniture. Now the settee is once again in an Italian palace.

• Recently when an estate in Wheeling, West Virginia, was being settled the lawyer for the estate took special notice of a carpet that had been used as a dust cover for a billiard table. To the lawyer, the carpet, which measured 12 feet 6 inches by 9 feet, seemed to be of particularly high quality. He photographed it and sent the color slide to Sotheby Parke Bernet in New York to see if the auction house could identify and appraise the carpet. The identification was that the carpet was a fine one, made of silk in the village of Heriz in northwest Persia. The carpet was beautiful and in fine condition, but barely an antique, since it was only 125 years old. Still, the auction house estimated that it would bring $40,000 to $60,000. As it turned out, the carpet set a record for any carpet sold at auction when it brought $200,000.

• In Murano, the factory center for the making of Venetian glassware, a single octagonal water glass or wine glass costs about $75. If six or more glasses are ordered, the price drops to $65 a glass. At the Rose D'Or commission mart in Darien, Connecticut, in 1975 an entire set of eighty-two old octagonal Venetian glasses was sold for $225—less than $3 a glass.

• In 1966 a 1955 Mercedes-Benz 300S convertible was sold in New York for $800. It needed paint, a new top, reupholstering, and some mechanical and chrome work. When the car was restored to like-new condition it represented a total investment of about $4,000. This car model has been rising steadily in price since that time. The November 1976 *Road and Track* magazine contained an advertisement of a 1955 Mercedes-Benz 300S convertible, even painted the same color as the one bought for $800. The price asked was $19,500.

One could go on and on about collectibles that resulted in wealth-building because of an advantageous purchase, or because the true nature of the item was not understood, or because the market rose far and fast.

Investing in antique furniture

In the previous chapter on investing in a home it was pointed out that we once placed bids on two large houses—and got them both. Since we had in storage less than enough furniture to fill one medium-sized home, it was necessary to purchase as rapidly as possible furnishings for a fifteen-room house and an eighteen-room house. We purchased some antiques, but with so many rooms to furnish, it was obvious that a huge sum of money would be needed to furnish both houses completely with antiques. The answer was to furnish them with a combination of new furniture, secondhand furniture purchased at auction and elsewhere, and medium-grade antiques found at reasonable prices. In the year we spent furnishing the two houses we bought well over 1,000 items of various kinds, mostly at the lesser auctions in New York City.

At the time we found a prospective buyer for the larger of the two houses we met with some resistance since the buyer owned a six-room cooperative apartment in New York City. The furniture in that apartment would not go very far toward furnishing an eighteen-room house.

After the purchase of the house was concluded the new owner started buying furnishings at auction, but also wanted to acquire some of the antiques we had purchased at auction during the previous year.

Among other items, we sold to the buyer of our home a fine Pennsylvania chest-on-chest, circa 1780, for $625. We also sold a Pennsylvania slant-top desk with ogee feet that we had bought from the family for whom it had been made in the eighteenth century. For this piece we received $350. A fine large Renaissance credenza of the seventeenth century we sold for $250.

The Boom in Prices
Of Antique Furniture

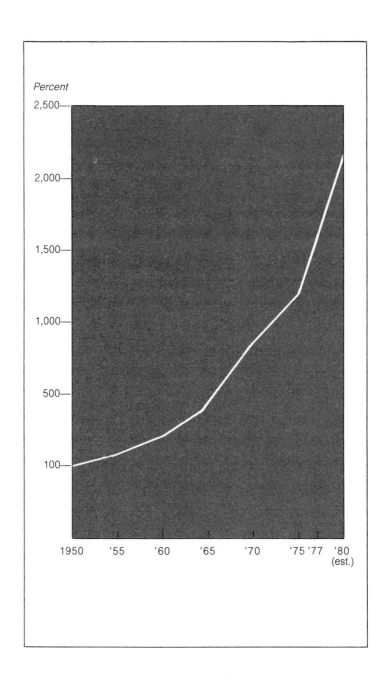

For everything we sold we received a check for a little over $6,000, which was 248 percent of our cost price one year earlier. We may have been smart investors in antiques, but so was the buyer of our house and our furniture. An antique dealer whom our buyer had known for many years arrived at the house one day with a check made out for the purchase of the chest-on-chest which we had sold for $625. The check for $5,000 was not accepted, and the chest-on-chest still stands in the house exactly where we placed it.

The slant-top desk, should the buyer wish to sell it today, would be worth at least $2,000—a far cry from the $350 we received for it.

The Renaissance credenza we sold for $250 would be worth a minimum of $2,500 today.

Of course the house itself is now worth about three times what we received for it.

Once in a while a very good buy can be made in antique furniture. Such a buy was made in 1969 at a sale in Washington, D.C., held by a lady who had bought a number of antiques in China in the mid-1920s. Included in the group of items offered was a four-part Chinese red lacquer dining table made around 1800. It had elaborate decorations in black lacquer over the red lacquer as well as scroll work. The two center sections were square and could be used separately as card tables or for other purposes. The two end sections were semicircular and could be used as console tables placed against the wall. When the entire table was put together, it measured over ten feet in length and could be used as a banquet table. We purchased the table for $2,500.

After moving into our new home in Greenwich, Connecticut, we gave a small tea party and invited a collector of Chinese red lacquer furniture to attend so that we could show off our purchase. We did not quite expect the collector's reaction. She offered ever-higher sums of money for the table as she said it would go well with her other

Chinese red lacquer pieces. At $15,000 she stopped, realizing that we had no intention of selling. Still, we were pleased that this collector confirmed our judgment in acquiring the table both as a beautiful and useful home decoration and as a prime investment.

If there are lessons to be learned from the above examples they are:

1. It is always possible—including right now—to buy collectibles that are rising in value and will continue to rise.

2. If you concentrate on becoming knowledgeable about one or two kinds of collectibles you will spot fine, genuine items offered for sale at auction and by dealers.

3. By reviewing auction sales catalogs with price lists and by visiting dealers you will become familiar with the market and market prices and will thus be able to buy intelligently with a view to price appreciation.

4. At almost every auction there is an item that goes at a bargain price because it does not attract bidders. Be on the lookout for such items.

Art as a source of income

An authority on stock market investments, Gerald Loeb, was one of the first to present an interesting and useful idea of how to realize on investments. He suggested selling a part of one's portfolio each year in order to meet living expenses. A part of the realization each year would be a return of capital, but another part would, it was hoped, be capital gain on the securities sold. Although capital would be spent, Mr. Loeb felt that the remaining portfolio would appreciate in value enough to offset the loss of the capital in the securities that were sold.

It might work like this: A person would, at the end of the year, sell $30,000 worth of securities that had cost $20,000. The capital gain would be $10,000, but the entire $30,000 would be spent for living expenses, including $20,000 of the capital—the original cost of the securities sold.

The objective would be to realize enough profit during the year on the portfolio to at least replace the loss of $20,000 in capital. The portfolio might be worth $300,000 at the end of the year in which 10 percent of it—$30,000 worth of securities—was sold. At the beginning of that year, however, the portfolio might have been worth only $260,000. During that year it would have appreciated $40,000, more than enough to replace the loss of $20,000 in capital. The year's appreciation would have been a little over 15 percent—a possible goal.

The next year the portfolio would have to appreciate enough to offset the amount taken out of capital and spent for that year—and so on for each year.

This theory can be applied to paintings or any other appreciating collectible, or to any collectible that has already appreciated in value. A person who paid $50,000 for a painting collection might well find today that it is worth $300,000. If the entire collection were sold for $300,000 net, the capital gain would be $250,000. The first $50,000 of capital gain would be taxed at 25 percent, but the other $200,000 would be taxed at 35 percent plus an amount up to or even higher than 5 percent, resulting in a total rate of 40 percent or more in taxes.

Thus, it might pay such an investor to sell only enough paintings each year to cover some living expenses and at the same time stay in a low capital gains tax bracket.

This writer started in a modest way to collect art in 1955 with the purchase of a seventeenth-century Dutch painting for $250 at the Flea Market in Arlington, Virginia. The shop owner was unaware of the painting's real worth.

Later in the 1950s this writer and his wife made other modest purchases of art. In the 1960s our collecting activities began to move into high gear. This emphasis on

How Paintings by Old Masters
Have Increased in Price

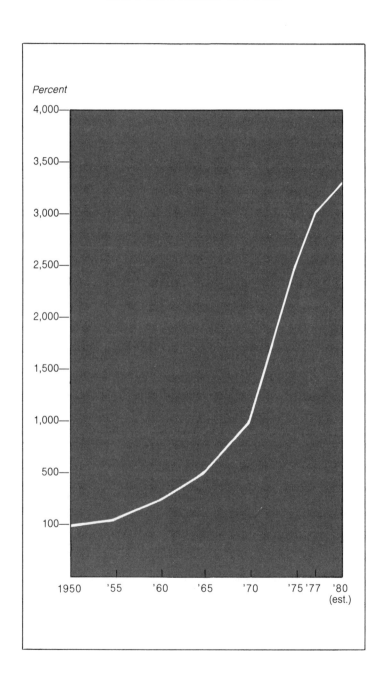

Percent

serious collecting became possible as we gained knowledge of art. Prior to the purchase of our first old master in
1955 neither of us had more than a general idea of either
old master paintings or their value, and this was the type
of painting on which we concentrated from 1960 on.

In 1973 the art market began to hit new highs and it
seemed wise for us to start selling. In December 1973 we
sold fourteen paintings through the Sotheby Parke Bernet Galleries in New York. The paintings had cost us a
total of $6,245. In the sale they realized $51,750. This was
eight and one-quarter times their cost, and we had
owned them an average of eight years. Our net return
after commissions was $45,505—over seven times our
original investment.

In June 1974 we sold more paintings, this time at Christie's in London, and the following December we sold still
more in London.

Our score for the three sales in which our twenty paintings were sold was a total selling price of $110,692.25 for
paintings that had cost us $11,145. The selling price rep-
resented 9.9 times the cost. Our holding period for these
paintings was eight years.

In June 1975 we sent more paintings to Christie's in
London for auctioning. The first was a Renaissance painting of a Madonna and Child by Jacopo del Sellaio. This
painting, 33½ by 23 inches, had been bought in 1966
from the New York firm of Galka and Roman for $2,500.
It was in reasonably good condition, but at some point in
its history it had been transferred to canvas after its original wood panel had deteriorated.

Christie's in London and this collector traced some of
this painting's history. It had once been in the Santa Bar-
bara Museum of Art in California and had also been on
loan to the Los Angeles County Museum of Art—two
facts which certainly did not hurt its value. The painting
was also listed by two authorities on Italian art—Bernard
Berenson and Raimond van Marle.

We felt that Christie's should accept no less than 2,500 pounds for the painting, which, considering the exchange rate on the pound sterling at the time, worked out to about $5,675. Christie's, however, thought that the "reserve," or minimum price, should be set at 2,000 pounds—$4,540. We agreed on this $4,540 reserve.

At the sale the painting brought 7,875 pounds sterling—$17,876—which was seven times its cost of $2,500.

The other painting sold in the same auction was by the seventeenth-century Dutch artist J. S. Mancadan. It was a religious picture—Christ and the woman of Samaria—which is not a universally popular type of art. The painting was on a wood panel and had somewhat deteriorated. It measured 44¼ by 32½ inches. We had bought the painting in the early 1970s for $2,300. At the June 1975 auction it realized 1,890 pounds—$4,290.

In the following year—on July 9, 1976—more of our paintings were offered for sale at Christie's in London. The first was a religious picture of striking beauty. It had been bought from a New York dealer for $3,600 in the mid-1960s. The artist was unknown at that time but the painting certainly was early Flemish. It depicted the Madonna and Child, Saint Joseph, and a cherub, and bore the date "1536." The painting measured 28 by 21½ inches. Later it was positively identified through our research as being by the so-called Master of the Half-Lengths, who was active in Bruges and Antwerp in the first half of the sixteenth century.

When one has a painting by an unknown master it is important to have a leading authority agree with one's attribution to a particular artist. In the case of this painting, its attribution to the "Master of the Half-Lengths" was upheld by the authority on Flemish art, Julius Held.

Christie's felt that a minimum price of 4,000 pounds should be placed on this painting. We disagreed and requested that the reserve be 6,000 pounds. By 1976 the pound had declined drastically in value from $2.27 in

1974 to $1.80, and we were interested in dollars rather than pounds. At the auction the painting brought 7,500 pounds—$13,500—about 3.8 times its cost.

The second of our pictures sold in the same sale was a seventeenth-century Dutch half-length portrait of a pretty woman. It was inscribed and dated "1638," and the inscription indicated that the woman's age was twenty-two. The painting measured 44½ by 33½ inches and, although on a wood panel, was in good condition.

The Netherlands Art Archives identified the artist as Thomas de Keyser, a prominent portraitist of seventeenth-century Holland. We had bought the painting in the late 1950s for $300 from a New York dealer. At the auction it realized 3,000 pounds, or $5,400—eighteen times its original cost.

The final picture we sold in this auction was a large Italian baroque painting of two figures, *Caritas* by Pietro Liberi, measuring 48 by 39½ inches. It had been bought at the Savoy Art and Auction Galleries in New York in the early 1960s for $350. In the 1976 sale it realized 800 pounds—$1,440—which is about four times its cost.

The check we received from Christie's after this sale was for $17,644.99. After deducting commissions, insurance, and freight on the three paintings we sold in this auction, as well as the original cost of the paintings, our profit amounted to $13,394.99.

So successful has been this policy of selling a limited number of paintings each year that we will probably follow the same procedure in the future. By selling some paintings each year, we accomplish several objectives. In the first place, and highly important, we secure an annual cash flow. It is possible that by regulating sales each year out of our "inventory" of paintings, we can live for years entirely on the proceeds of the paintings sold.

By selling a limited number of paintings each year, capital gains are held to $50,000 or less, and the capital gains tax is 25 percent rather than 35 percent or more.

By selling a limited number of paintings, we still have pictures to adorn our home and to enjoy. And it is much easier to replace, say, three paintings sold each year than it would be to acquire replacements for fifteen or twenty paintings in one year.

Also, it is, of course, important to realize profits while profits are possible. As of early 1977 it seems that paintings of the older schools of art will never decline in value and that they may possibly continue to rise. Still, some types of collectibles that brought high prices in the past have decreased in value during more recent times.

How it was done

Originally we purchased paintings because (1) they were beautiful and of fine quality; (2) they would add to the decor of our home; and (3) they were inexpensive— most of them costing under $1,000, many of them costing under $500, and some even costing $100 or less.

An important factor in our decision to buy these pictures was that they were old master paintings, none more recent than the eighteenth century. We felt that age alone gave them value, or at least potential value.

The paintings, while very low in price, were obviously limited in supply if none of them was newer than the eighteenth century; and our particular interest, seventeenth-century Dutch art, was a century older. If there were any increase in demand for these paintings the demand would have to be satisfied out of a very limited supply. Thus we felt that the prices might rise.

Actually, as we began to be interested in these paintings prices were rising, although not much each year. The low cost per painting, plus the fact that the paintings were rising in price, meant that the "downside risk" was small. We were not buying a Monet for $50,000. We were buying a de Keyser for $300. How much could we lose? And if prices should decline, we would still have our home decorated with beautiful works of art.

Early in our collecting we found that a number of paintings on the market for reasonable sums of money were by masters represented in major museums. A Nicolaes Maes that we bought for $1,800 was not only a beautiful painting, but other paintings by Maes were to be found in many major art galleries of the world, including the Rijksmuseum, Holland's finest art gallery.

We felt that a major type of collectible was being overlooked by collectors and investors, and that the situation would eventually change, which it did.

Purely from an investment point of view, we timed our sales so that each year we secured some income plus some return of capital. The capital gain was taxed essentially at half the rate of ordinary income. We might have sold everything at once, but had we done this we would have gone into the 35-percent-plus capital gains tax bracket, whereas our maximum capital gains tax was always 25 percent or less.

So perhaps we unconsciously followed the investment advice of Gerald Loeb to sell enough of the "portfolio" each year to pay one's bills and hope the rest of the portfolio rose enough to offset the capital taken out of it for living expenses.

Investing in wines

While continuing to invest in art, this writer added another type of collectible to his "portfolio." His entry into this new field began at a party in New York in early 1968 when he engaged in a conversation with Dr. Roland de Marco, chairman of the Korean-American Foundation. This writer knew of Dr. de Marco's interest in wines and thought it would be an opportunity to learn about them since he knew nothing about any kind of wine. The opening to the subject came as the result of a 1959 wine the host and hostess served. This writer wanted to know from Dr. de Marco something about the wine and learned that it had been produced in one of the best vintage years of all time in France. Whatever it cost the host of the dinner party in 1968, it would probably cost at least three times that much today.

One result of the conversation with Dr. de Marco was that we began to buy wines—first, to see how fine wines tasted, and second, to "invest" in vintage French wines, if this were possible. A modest number of bottles was therefore purchased for our home in Washington, D.C.

Each summer we went on a trip to Europe. Canterbury, in the county of Kent, England, was always a visiting place, and across from the hotel was a small wine shop, B. C. Blyth and Company. This shop had been there for centuries and its appearance must have been about the same in 1769 as it was in 1969 when we first visited it.

The owner of the shop, Mr. A. M. Tee, was more than willing to educate us on the subject of vintage wines, and the result was a series of purchases of what seemed to be fine vintage French wines at reasonable prices.

Each time we visited Canterbury we purchased a case or two of fine wines and left them in the cellar of the shop.

Soon we began to feel that we were developing a collection, if only a modest one. At the time one of the finest vintage wines obtainable was Château Lafite-Rothschild 1959. Since Mr. Tee did not have this wine, we timed one of our trips from Washington to visit one of Christie's wine auctions in London where a case of Lafite-Rothschild 1959 was being offered for sale. We bought the case of Lafite in the summer of 1971 for $205. We also continued to buy from Mr. Tee whatever seemed to be quality wine offered at reasonable prices.

By the fall of 1972 vintage French wine had risen greatly in price and we instructed Mr. Tee to ship all of our wines that were in his cellar to Christie's in London to be auctioned. We also instructed Christie's to offer our case of Lafite 1959 for sale.

The auction of our wines was a considerable success.

The Appreciation in Prices
Of Vintage Burgundy and Bordeaux Wines

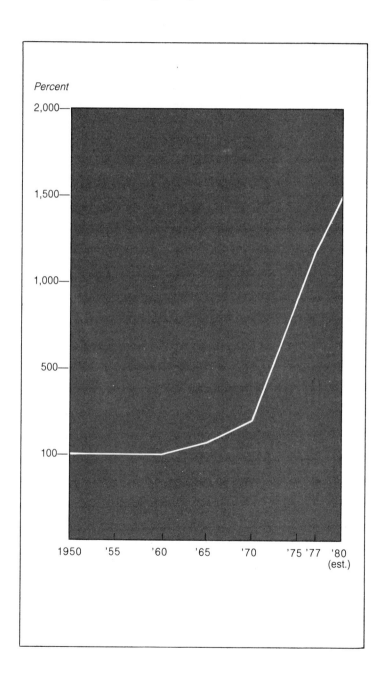

Less than a year before the sale we had bought from Mr. Tee a case (twelve bottles to the case) of Château Margaux 1952 for $178.50. It brought at auction $350—1.9 times its cost. At the same time we bought the Margaux 1952 we bought a case of Château Latour 1952, also for $178.50. This case realized $325—1.8 times its cost. We sold a case of Château Latour 1959, which had cost us $131.20, for $450—3.4 times its cost. Two cases of the great Burgundy wine Domaine Romanée-Conti had cost us $165 a case—$330 in all, and they contained magnums (double-size bottles) of the vintage year 1964. The two cases realized $1,000 at auction—three times their cost. A case of twelve assorted bottles of wines of the vintage years 1949 to 1959 brought $312.50—2.8 times their cost of $109.66.

The Château Lafite-Rothschild that had cost $205 we sold for $775 for the case of twelve bottles—3.75 times what we had paid a year and a half earlier.

A few months prior to this sale we had purchased six half-bottles of Mouton-Rothschild 1955 for $43.50. They brought $78—1.8 times their cost.

The haulage from Canterbury to London was supplied gratis by B. C. Blyth and Company. There was a very small storage cost in London. After Christie's had deducted their commission for selling the wine, we received a check for $2,992.21—approximately three times what the wines had cost us. The term of our "investment" was an average of two and a half years.

This return was certainly not a very large sum of money. On the other hand, we had invested very little in the wine. We bought as we could—whenever we found fine vintage French wines at reasonable prices. We bought not only in England but in the United States, and, with the exception of the case of Lafite-Rothschild 1959, we always bought from dealers.

If we ever decide to sell the rest of our wines, which are now in the United States, we will ship them to London for auction. From our present investment of about $7,000 we would expect to net about $25,000 after freight and selling commissions. Our average holding period is now about eight years. We have in the collection some prime wines—Château d'Yquem 1959, 1961, 1962, and 1966; Château Lafite-Rothschild 1955, 1961, and 1962; Château Margaux, Château Mouton-Rothschild, and Château Latour of the great vintage year 1959; and Domaine Romanée-Conti 1959, 1962, 1966, and 1967— among many other wines that have appreciated in value and that can easily be auctioned in London at a profit.

Collecting for pleasure and profit

If you decide to invest in collectibles you may wish to adopt the following course of action, which has proven to be effective for other investors:

1. Find out the answers to these two questions: What is rising in buyer interest and price? What seems to be a good buy simply because it is low in price in relation to other collectibles, to its past price, and in the minds of collectors and dealers familiar with the collectible?

Talk to dealers and auction officials to learn the answers to these questions. You can spend several weeks just visiting auction houses and dealers, talking about the things they are offering for sale and seeing what items interest them the most.

Be prepared to find a few dealers who will invite you to leave their shops. Unless you virtually have cash in your hand to make a purchase they will not talk. These dealers are in the minority. Most dealers, if they see that you are sincerely interested in developing a collection, will tell you about prices and trends.

Read newspapers to learn more about what is of buyer interest and what seems to be rising in price. In the old car area, all that you need do is to check the prices of old cars offered each Sunday in the *New York Times.* At your library old issues of the autos-for-sale section of the *Times* will show you that car prices have risen greatly in the past year.

By the same method, of course, you can see what is happening to prices of residential real estate and of many other commodities, not simply collectibles.

From such a survey you cannot help but learn a few things about collectibles, some facts of use to you and some not. In the autumn of 1976 you would have found, for instance, that impressionist paintings were by no means in a price boom. Neither were French moderns, probably not even Picasso. You would also have found that nonrealistic contemporary art was certainly not booming.

On the other hand, you would have learned that first-grade old masters were strong in price. So were nineteenth-century Continental, English, and American landscapes.

You would have found that eighteenth-century British portraits were rising but were certainly in no boom.

You would have found that eighteenth-century English and American furniture was rising well in price.

You would have found that while fine eighteenth-century French furniture was high in price and "holding," nineteenth-century imitations of this great furniture were in something of a boom.

2. Collect what interests you. A great collectible has been the "penny fairings," those little toy novelties given away or sold for a penny or so at English fairs about a century ago and also more recently. These are not works of art but their price rise at auction has been phenomenal. Still, they have limited collector appeal, and those interested in Louis XV furniture or fine Chinese ceramics might well not be interested in such simple little collectibles.

If you collect what is of no interest to you simply to make money, you will soon find that the whole collecting

activity is distasteful even though profitable. In that
event it is quite possible you will not have the sustained
interest necessary for finding items that will make your
collection a success.

3. Collect what you can afford. You may not be financially in a position to collect Louis XV furniture or impressionist paintings, but you may well be able to afford
prints, lithos, Venetian glass, eighteenth-century American and English furniture, or an old car—perhaps a Jag-
uar XK120 roadster.

The first investment that this writer made was the purchase of a Rolls-Royce Phantom I Riviera town car right
after graduating from college. The car cost $550. His sav-
ings amounted to $350, and he borrowed $200 from a
bank in New York at an annual interest rate of 2 percent.
He was "credit-worthy" since he had a good job with a
big company which paid him $1,620 a year! The car was
financed in this way and soon sold at a good profit. Of
course, had he held the car until 1977 he could have sold
it for about $50,000.

4. Collect what you can find. You may like Elizabethan
furniture, but how much of it can you find to purchase?
The same is true for sixteenth-century Italian furniture.
Seventeenth-century furniture is much the same as that
of the sixteenth century but vastly more plentiful. Avoid
trying to collect items that are too scarce to permit you to
form a collection.

5. Try to collect things that are sold at auction, for several reasons:

If the collectibles you are interested in are sold at auction you will be able to buy them at such sales, and you
need not hunt for them in dealers' shops. This is particularly advisable if you do not have a great deal of spare
time to pursue your collecting activities.

If you can buy your collectible at auction, you can also
sell it at auction. You can thus take a profit on the sale
and your liquidity will be improved. You do not want to

Antique and Classic Cars
Rising Fast in Value

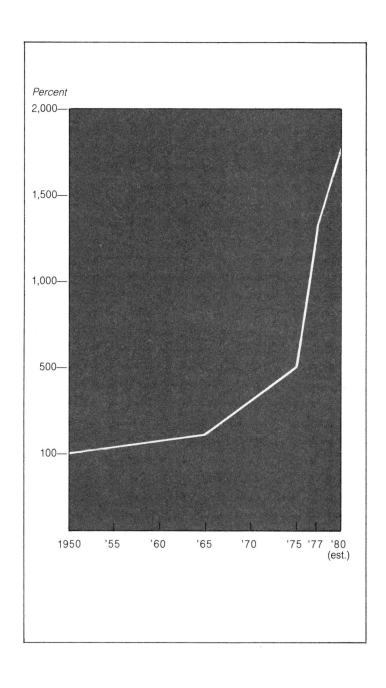

sink a great deal of money in collectibles that can be only slowly, or perhaps never, liquidated. Steam yachts are a fine collectible, but they are not as easy to sell as nineteenth-century American landscape paintings.

If your collectible is sold at auction you will have an auction price to guide you in buying and selling.

6. Follow prices very closely to see how much you should pay for collectibles, what you should sell them for, and what the market is doing.

The main way to follow prices of collectibles is to secure auction catalogs. These are often on file in public libraries or art museums. This particular collector has spent weeks, and even months, collecting and recording prices of art and antiques for a period of years in order to determine price trends.

7. Study auction catalogs to see what is offered, at what prices, what characteristics give the collectible value, and what detracts from value.

8. Early in your collecting do not put a great deal of money into any one item or into your total collection. Too many people with little knowledge caught collection fever in the bull market for collectibles in 1973, particularly in the painting market. On May 2, 1973, Paul Cézanne's *Vase de Tulipes*, 28 by 16½ inches, on paper mounted on board, sold at auction in New York for $1.4 million. In the same sale *Nature Morte aux Poissons*, 17½ by 28¼ inches, by Edouard Manet, sold for an identical sum. With such high purchase prices, one might find it hard to sell at a future date for sums of this magnitude, and it would be even more difficult to sell for a profit.

Go slowly and put a limit on the amount you spend for any one item.

It is not at all a precept of collecting that the more you pay for an item the surer it is to rise in price. A good case might be made for the exactly opposite conclusion.

9. Buy the very best quality you can find for the price you want to pay. This means that the item should be a

fine example of its type, not a mediocre thing; and it should be in good condition in relation to its age.

10. Become knowledgeable about authenticity. It is very easy to be fooled by fakes. In the past we have undertaken to advise buying English watercolors. The kind we recommended buying is little subject to faking since such watercolors sell for under $100 apiece, some of them selling for under $50 or even under $25. Who would bother to fake them? If you do buy a fake you have bought a $50 or $100 fake, not a $10,000 fake.

Dealers will usually be glad to help you to distinguish the genuine from the false in paintings and in antiques. So will the personnel at auction houses.

11. You might buy from reputable dealers who will take back things that are not "right" and may even give a guarantee of authenticity. The London dealer who unwittingly sold fake English watercolors recently has a reputation for making good on anything the buyer returns, fake or otherwise.

12. As your expertise develops, buy from smaller dealers and from auctions. In this way you may be able to secure a price advantage as compared with the prices of the larger dealers—but certainly not always. Remember that dealers buy things at auction to resell at higher prices. You pay for their expertise in buying.

13. Try to form a collection. A good and balanced collection is of more interest to a dealer or an auction house than one item.

If you go to a big auction house to sell one old master painting, it may be accepted for sale. On the other hand, if you have a good collection of fifteen old masters, you may find the auction house eager to have it and willing to make concessions to you on the rate of commission, on the cost of illustrations, and on the charge for the buy-backs of items that do not sell.

If you have a big collection, the auction house may even conduct the sale at your home, so that haulage to the auction house is not required—and breakage is likely to be less.

14. Find out who are the leading dealers in your collectible and cultivate them. They will keep you abreast of the market and will authenticate and value items for you—even items scheduled for auction. You will, however, have to pay them for their services and/or buy things from them occasionally. Most of our own paintings, incidentally, have been bought from dealers, and many from leading London dealers; so dealer prices are certainly not always above auction prices.

15. Make friends with other collectors in your field, and trade information with them, particularly on where items of interest may be purchased. You cannot buy everything you see, even though the items may be offered at bargain prices. So give other collectors opportunities and tips, and you may get back as much as, or more than, you give.

16. Find out who are the experts in your field of collecting. If you are interested in Italian paintings, you will learn that leading experts in the United States are Robert and Bertina Manning, Anthony Clark, and Everett Fahy. The Kunsthistorisches Institut in Florence, Italy, is both helpful and authoritative in identifying artists who painted Italian pictures. It is difficult to sell an Italian painting, at least an old master, in Italy unless its authenticity has been approved by the late Antonio Morassi.

The Netherlands Art Archives in The Hague can help to identify unknown artists of Dutch paintings from photographs sent them, and they do on-the-spot counseling.

In the field of autographs, there is possibly no greater authority than auctioneer Charles Hamilton of New York.

For stamps, a leading authority is Bernard D. Harmer of the H. R. Harmer auction house in New York.

Very often the person who wrote the definitive work about a particular artist is a great authority on the subject, such as Rodolfo Pallucchini on the artist Titian.

17. Consider where to keep your collectibles. This question leads back to picking your collectibles in the first place. Just prior to World War II a top official of Western Union invested in fine antique furniture. Soon there was too much for his home and he began to store it in warehouses. The furniture turned out to be a fine collectible, as the antique furniture market in 1939 was at rock bottom, particularly the market for fine French antiques.

An investment in such a collection of antique furniture today would require a major outlay for acquisition plus costly storage fees and insurance. However, furniture that you can use in your home is an ideal collectible if it does not overflow into warehouses.

Foreign warehouses are often less expensive than those in the United States. Some dealers will store things for buyers, both in this country and abroad. We have left furniture in storage for a long time in Italy and in England. Wine dealers have stored purchases for us for years—at no charge. When we did pay for wine storage (at controlled temperatures) in London the cost was extremely modest.

18. Consider the international market. A collectible that has an international market is vastly to be preferred over one that has only an American market. In the 1973-74 recession the American collector was buying very little. On the other hand Mideastern demand, Japanese demand, and European demand did not slacken. In fact, it increased in some areas and prices rose. If the American dollar declines in value, you may want to sell in a country whose currency is rising. The British pound was low in late 1976; the German mark was rising. British dealer demand for collectibles was not the strongest; German demand was felt in a number of collectible fields.

19. Consider a collectible for the whole family, not just for yourself. If a great deal of money is spent on collecting, the other members of the family may object. If the whole family approves of it and participates in the col-

lecting activity, it should result in a happier situation.

By choosing a collecting activity of interest to the entire family, such as furniture, carpets, or paintings, your home can be beautified while a potentially profitable collection is acquired.

20. Set up a collecting budget. At the outset it should be decided whether funds for collecting are to come out of income or out of capital. There is nothing wrong with putting capital into collectibles. Many investments in collectibles have worked out just as well as investments in the stock market—or better.

On the other hand, you do not have to worry so much about losses on collectibles purchased out of income. As the collecting activity develops, however, and as your knowledge of the collectible and its market increases, it will almost inevitably turn into an investment medium that involves more money than income can provide. There is nothing to fear in this development—if your collecting is done with as much careful research and good judgment as you would use in buying securities.

7

Organizing
a Business—
and
Selling It

The best piece of business advice this writer has ever heard came not from a tycoon but from clergyman Norman Vincent Peale. He advised: "Find a need and fill it." A new business is most likely to succeed if it is based on that simple concept.

Those who would like to go into business for themselves may think this advice is easy to give and hard to follow. Where, they may ask, could there possibly be a need that is not adequately filled by the thousands of businesses already in existence?

Such needs vary with the times, and one must be alert to profit from them. As just one current example, a "runaway" business is the installation of burglar-alarm systems in the suburbs. One such contractor—not a manufacturer, but simply a contractor—experienced a 650 percent gain in business in the Connecticut suburbs close to New York City in the first six months of 1976. The firm cannot keep up with the demand for installations even though it charges 50 percent of the total cost in advance of starting any work. These advance payments are being used as the company's working capital. Right now, the big fear in suburban communities is break-ins, and the firm is taking full advantage of this new market.

Filling a need

To see exactly how another need was recognized and successfully filled we shall go back some years to the time when this writer was approached by an insurance company to become a field representative on a commission basis. The firm insured automobiles, but wanted to enter the mobile home field in the belief that it would be at least as profitable as insuring cars.

The company officials offered this writer 3 percent of all premiums received from the mobile home industry. They also proposed something unique. They would assist every mobile home dealer to get an insurance agent's license so that the dealer could receive commissions on all insurance business coming from the dealership.

The proposal appeared to be a good one from the point of view of the dealers. A dealer who sold a mobile home and wrote insurance on it was assured of both the usual business profit plus a commission from the insurance company.

This plan, however, did not have much appeal for most of the dealers. While they liked the idea of increased profits through commissions on insurance covering the mobile homes they sold, they were much more concerned with a big obstacle to selling the mobile homes. The problem was that few people then had the cash to buy mobile homes. They might have had the cash when a mobile home cost about $1,500, but not when the price rose to $5,000 or more.

There were, of course, finance plans of banks and other financial institutions to help prospective owners buy more easily through time payments. The usual plan was one-third down, three years to pay, and 6 percent annual interest. One-third of $1,500 is $500 down, and the remaining $1,000 over three years comes to a little under $33 a month, interest included. The $5,000 mobile home was vastly more burdensome to the purchaser, however. A buyer would have to pay one-third of $5,000 down—$1,667—and would then have to make monthly payments of about $110, including interest.

In addition to the unsuitability of the plan of one-third down and three years to pay that was standard throughout the mobile home industry, the country was in a recession at the time and banks and finance companies were not at all anxious to get into any of the newer fields of financing.

There was thus a scarcity of finance to meet the needs of the industry. In some cases dealers had no finance plans available to them. They could only sell for cash or not sell at all.

It became clear that this writer, trying to establish a business, was barking up the wrong tree. What was needed to sell to the mobile home dealers—something that they would buy—was a workable, up-to-date finance plan that buyers could afford.

This was the plan worked out after many trials and errors: one-quarter down instead of one-third down, and the balance to be paid over five years instead of three years. The interest was to be 5 percent instead of 6 percent. A dealer who chose to charge more interest would get the difference between 5 percent and whatever rate was charged.

In business, contacts are often made in unexpected places. At a cocktail party in Washington, D.C., this writer began talking to a gentleman who said he was connected with a bank. The mobile home finance plan was explained in some detail to this chance acquaintance. The discussion continued at a restaurant after the party.

At the end of the evening the gentleman said, "I like the plan. Our bank will go into it with you. You develop the dealer business for us and you will write all of the insurance on all of the mobile homes we finance."

At that point the gentleman was asked what exactly he did in the bank. He replied, "I'm the head of the bank."

The next step was to get a place in which to conduct the business. A relative kindly offered her vacant apartment. The understanding was that if our business succeeded we would pay her $125 a month retroactive to the date we moved into the apartment. If the business did not succeed, we would owe her nothing.

We bought an old desk for $15 and refinished it ourselves. Above the desk we mounted what was called by the manufacturer a "pin-up light." It cost $2.50. For another $15 we secured a secondhand typewriter, and we were in business.

We launched the business in May of one year. By the end of the year we obviously had not made much money as our federal income tax for the year amounted to only $625.42.

The next year was quite different. We received premiums of about $500,000 and our taxable income was $55,000. It might be mentioned that we wrote what was called retrospective insurance, which held out the hope of a very high commission rate provided losses were low for the insured mobile homes over a period of years.

Not long afterward we incorporated our insurance agency and received 100,000 shares of the new corporation. This stock we swapped for the stock of a finance company, after first securing an opinion from the Internal Revenue Service that the stock swap would be tax-free. The stock that we received we later sold for over $2 a share—more than $200,000 in all. The finance company had been willing to swap stock in anticipation of the insurance agency's future profits—nothing else. We did not include so much as a typewriter in the deal. We in effect capitalized our earnings, which is the same as "created goodwill." The valuation of this stream of earnings is always done in the sale of business organizations.

This was a small business enterprise. Now let us look at a very large one.

Building an organization

George Delacorte set up a publishing company in New York in 1922 with a few thousand dollars—as many businesses are started. The business prospered and he became a leading publisher of paperback books. He thought about selling the business on and off for many years. Several years ago he refused an offer of twelve times annual earnings for his business.

In 1975 he thought about selling out again, but in that recession year all he was offered for the business was six times earnings. He felt that this capitalization-of-earnings figure was too low. Nevertheless, even six times earnings would have resulted in a sales price very much in excess of the value of the physical assets owned by the publishing company.

Then, in 1976, Mr. Delacorte received what he considered a fine offer. Again, this offer was based strictly on annual earnings produced by the company over a period of years. The price was twenty-two and one-half times annual earnings. The settlement price was paid by the buying company in cash—$37 million.

The above two examples are of businesses built from nothing with the end result a fine capital gain. The first was accomplished quickly; the second, over a period of many years. The first business buildup and sale required hard work but no particular expertise, education, or experience. The second became a major organization in the publishing field with many highly trained and experienced personnel.

Let us now discuss some of the simpler types of businesses that can be used to build capital.

Creating and selling goodwill

It is not difficult to locate businesses for sale which are almost 100 percent goodwill and which have a value dependent solely upon weekly or monthly earnings. One need only read the "Business Opportunities" section of a large daily newspaper to find such offerings. What the business is worth on the market depends on little more than how much it earns.

Several years ago a morning newspaper route in Brooklyn, New York, was offered for sale. About 800 copies of newspapers, including the *New York Times*, were delivered seven days a week on this route. The owner of the business was franchised by the newspapers, and the franchise would remain his exclusively as long as he delivered the papers satisfactorily.

The route had been built up gradually. One of the most important functions that the owner of the route performed, in addition to acquiring the customers in the first place, was the weeding out of slow-paying and nonpaying customers, so that the route consisted of 800 good customers, not simply 800 customers.

Three men had to be employed in order to deliver the newspapers each day. They began work at 5:30 A.M. and continued until all the deliveries had been made, for which each man received $30 to $35 a week. After the papers had been delivered the men went to their regular full-time jobs.

The owner of the route arrived at a central point at 5:30 A.M. to receive the papers from the newspaper companies' delivery trucks. He then distributed the papers to the deliverymen. If one of the deliverymen was absent, the route owner secured a substitute. By 6:30 A.M. the route owner was finished with his work and could go home. He thus worked an hour each morning and also

Types of Businesses in U.S.

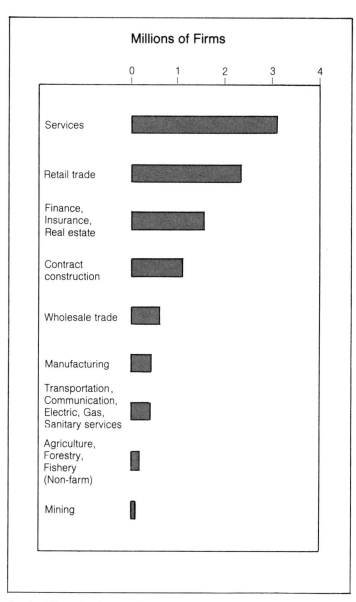

Millions of Firms

| | 0 | 1 | 2 | 3 | 4 |

Services

Retail trade

Finance, Insurance, Real estate

Contract construction

Wholesale trade

Manufacturing

Transportation, Communication, Electric, Gas, Sanitary services

Agriculture, Forestry, Fishery (Non-farm)

Mining

Note: In addition to these businesses there are over 3.1 million farms and 110,300 uncategorized firms, making a total of nearly 13 million businesses. Of this total, only about 350,000 are classified as large businesses.

Sources: Internal Revenue Service, Small Business Administration

took care of the billings. His regular nine-to-five job was that of manufacturer's representative.

The average year-round net income of the business, after all expenses, was $275 per week—in the summer a little less and in the winter a little more. The average had been brought up to this figure from $240 a week in the preceding year. Thus the business appeared to be growing. The $275 per week works out to an annual net income subject to taxation of about $14,000.

The owner's asking price for this business was $26,000, of which $10,000 was required as a cash down payment. The $16,000 balance was subject to negotiation as to the number of years during which it would be paid off. Actually the entire balance might almost have been paid off in one year out of the business's earnings except that income tax on the $14,000 net would have had to be paid.

The important thing to note in these details about this prosaic business is what was being sold for $26,000. Absolutely no assets were included in the purchase price, not even carts that the newspaper deliverers could load the papers onto and pull along their respective routes. The entire $26,000 was payment for the capitalization of earnings and goodwill.

Of course the buyer would have to perform services for one hour a day and take care of the billings, so some charge for his labor might theoretically be made against the $14,000 yearly profits. A small part of the income was, in other words, payment for the owner's services.

For the seller the $26,000 received was a capital gain realized simply through the building up of a business, not by selling something that had cost him a certain number of dollars and represented a tangible asset. The same principles of the valuation of earnings and goodwill apply to many other businesses, a few of which are: routes of all kinds, among them bread, other foods, and trash collection; gasoline stations; stores, particularly franchised liquor stores; and telephone answering services.

Implementing a unique idea

A number of years ago Bankers Development Corporation was organized by Jerome E. Casey and operated in New York. The corporation did two things: It solicited savings accounts for various banks, and for this service the corporation received a fee from the bank. Its more significant purpose, however, was to install in banks the "Thrifti-Check Service Plan," a personalized check service for depositors.

The services that Bankers Development Corporation performed were installing the system in the bank, instructing the bank employees in its operation, supervising the system until the bank employees could operate it by themselves, and supplying the forms, checkbooks, covers, passbooks, promotional booklets, pamphlets, counter cards, lobby posters, and newspaper advertising mats. Bankers Development Corporation also supplied to the banks checkbook stapling machines and printing presses for putting the depositors' names on the checks.

The usual contract for supplying such services to a bank had a duration of five years, and the corporation had such contracts with 200 banks.

Bankers Development Corporation was liquidated in 1953, and its sole owner, Jerome E. Casey, acquired all the assets, which he then sold to the former president of the company and a few employees. The selling price was about $340,000 but the price is not so important. Of much more importance is what the purchasers bought:

Inventory	$20,589.73
Office furniture	9,183.09
Notes receivable	11,000.00
Unearned advance and sales accounts	2,600.00
Trademark and goodwill	5,000.00
Customer obligations	1,687.50
Contracts with banks	290,818.61

The $290,818.61 is the most significant item. It is the "going business" value, as the Tax Court described it. It is the goodwill or capitalization of earnings. The $5,000 item listed as "Trademark and goodwill" is to all intents and purposes the same thing.

Besides this payment to Mr. Casey, he was to receive $12,500 a year for life. This one operation had built him a fund of wealth sufficient to last him for the rest of his days.

Capitalizing on talent

This is the story of Julius H. ("Groucho") Marx, and the quotes are from the Tax Court of the United States:

"For many years . . . Marx had been a theatrical performer on the stage and in motion pictures. He had been a member of a team which consisted of him and his four brothers. In the early 1940s the team disbanded after several unsuccessful motion pictures. Thereafter . . . Marx appeared alone in one motion picture which was not successful. Prior to the fall of 1947 he had appeared in several radio shows which were unsuccessful. In the summer of 1947 he was not employed in any entertainment activities. On July 14 of that year he auditioned unsuccessfully for the job as quizmaster of the 'Take It or Leave It' radio quiz show."

At this juncture it would appear that Groucho Marx was finished in show business.

"John B. Guedel was first employed in the radio entertainment industry in the spring of 1937. His job was with a local Los Angeles advertising company as a joke writer. He later wrote dramatic shows and originated the singing commercial."

In the fall of 1947, Marx and Guedel collaborated in developing a radio show which they called "You Bet Your Life." Guedel paid about $250 to have a sample performance recorded. Then Marx and Guedel took the recording to the Illinois Watch Case Company to see whether the firm was interested in sponsoring the show. The company was interested and the show was booked for twenty-six weeks beginning in November 1947 from 8:00 to 8:30 P.M. on the American Broadcasting Company (ABC) network. The show ran through 1949 but was only moderately successful.

In 1949 the Illinois Watch Case Company switched the show to the Columbia Broadcasting System (CBS). There it became more successful. By the spring of 1950 it was one of the most popular shows on the air. In order to improve the show, Marx and Guedel got the Illinois Watch Case Company to release them, whereupon they secured the sponsorship of the DeSoto-Plymouth Dealers of America on CBS, Wednesdays from 9:00 to 9:30 P.M.

In May 1960 the two men decided to sell the show, and they invited CBS and the National Broadcasting Company (NBC) to submit sealed bids. Of the sales price, 75 percent was to go to Marx and 25 percent to Guedel. NBC won the show with a bid of $1 million plus the following weekly pay scale for Marx and Guedel:

	Marx	Guedel
First and second weeks	$4,750	$1,500
Third week	$5,000	$1,550
Fourth week	$5,100	$1,600
Fifth week	$5,100	$1,650
Option period	$5,700	$1,800

In addition, Marx was to receive $25,000 a year for five years and Guedel was to receive $15,000 a year for five years for their services as consultants.

The most significant thing about this transaction is the capital gains feature. Of the $1 million sales price, Marx received $750,000 and Guedel $250,000. Their cost bases for these capital gains were $658.19 for Marx and $109.42 for Guedel. The sale resulted in a gain for the partners subject to the then only 25 percent capital gains tax.

Of course many persons interested in building wealth might well point out that they do not have Groucho Marx's talent. Still they may have abilities in other directions or a certain amount of expertise developed over a period of time, perhaps a relatively short time, which can be used to build wealth.

Building capital from contacts

In the mobile home industry one insurance agent developed quite a reputation for promoting dealer business for banks and finance companies. He did this by mail advertising as well as by visiting dealers throughout the East by automobile. The dealers sent in their applications prepared by would-be mobile home purchasers on the time-payment plan. These time-payment contracts turned out to be very solid credits resulting in few losses, and they carried a satisfactory rate of interest for the banks and finance companies.

One day the president of a failing finance company visited the office of the insurance agent to make a proposition. The finance company was in the small loan field and many of these loans had turned sour, with the result that the company had been operating at a loss for a long time and had gone through a good deal of its capital. The president of the finance company felt that if the insurance agent could get the company out of small loans and into mobile home financing it would quickly turn a loss situation into a profitable one. In return for the agent's help, the president, who owned 100 percent of the company's voting stock, would sell the insurance man one-half of this stock for $500. The insurance man accepted the offer. Why not? All he had to lose was $500.

In less than a year after the deal took place the finance company was out of small loans and completely into mobile home financing—and completely in the black.

The insurance agent had a certain amount of expertise in the mobile home business, but not a great deal, and he had accumulated this knowledge during a period of four years. In a way he could control dealer business, but the control was more nominal than real. He knew the dealers and had secured them suitable bank and finance company connections to meet the time-sales finance needs of their customers. He simply informed the dealers of the new finance company in the mobile home field that used to be in small loans. The terms this company offered the mobile home dealers were competitive, but no more than that.

Exactly eighteen months after acquiring the finance company stock for $500 the insurance agent sold it for $125,000 cash.

Essentially this capital gain was accomplished by a man who had a group of dealer followers. Very often if a person "controls" business in this way it is an advantage in making business connections that result in income. In this case the contacts resulted in a large capital gain as well as income.

Businesses built from little or nothing

We have now considered in detail six different businesses and can classify them by their nature:

Business No. 1. The specialized insurance agency—finding a need and filling it.

Business No. 2. The publishing company—slowly but soundly building an organization.

Business No. 3. The newspaper route—creating a capital asset by plain hard work over a relatively short period of time.

Business No. 4. The personalized check company—implementing a unique idea.

Business No. 5. The radio show—capitalizing on one's talent.

Business No. 6. The specialized finance company—capitalizing on one's contacts and ability to control business.

To summarize how the businesses were started, how they grew, and how they resulted in capital:

1. Each of these businesses was started with either little capital or no capital.

The insurance agency was started with no capital. The first cash that came in was a check from a bank representing the premiums on several policies covering mobile homes financed by the bank. It was this premium check that opened the bank account of the insurance agency.

The Tax Court of the United States indicated that John Guedel had spent $250 to record a sample radio show, which sold the Illinois Watch Case Company on the idea of sponsoring the show. The Tax Court also found that the capital base of Groucho Marx in the entire enterprise that was sold for $1 million was $658.19 and John Guedel's capital base was $109.42.

The finance company was launched in the mobile home field with a $500 purchase of stock that was sold the following year for $125,000.

2. The experience of the organizers of most of the businesses was extremely limited.

The book publisher had had no experience in book publishing at all.

The insurance agent had never insured anything in his life. In order to operate the insurance agency he and his wife had to study booklets about insuring and pass tests to obtain life insurance and casualty insurance agents' licenses.

The $500 investor in the stock of the failing finance company had never had any experience in the field of finance.

3. In almost every case the buildup of the business was rapid.

It is true that the book publisher was in business for decades, but the business was a great success within ten years after being launched. In fact, all through the Great

Depression the company grew, unlike most other businesses in the United States.

4. In each of the six businesses the buildup culminated in a sale which produced a substantial amount of capital. Certainly the capital received in each case would have been hard, if not impossible, to acquire by working for a paycheck, paying taxes on annual earnings, and saving.

5. The sale of the majority of these businesses was of capitalized earnings or goodwill, not tangible assets.

The book publishing business involved the sale of some assets, but these assets were not great in relation to the sales price of the business.

6. In almost every case the sales price represented a very high "multiplier."

The price paid for the book publishing business was twenty-two and one-half times annual earnings.

7. In some cases the purchase price bought prestige and other benefits since the buyer could immediately control a good amount of wealth plus a going business, and could get on the payroll for a substantial salary as the head of the organization.

8. The seller often had added compensation too.

One seller remained as president of the company for some time. Several others had contracts that provided them with consultants' fees for a period of time.

9. In some cases the amount of capital received was large enough for the sellers to be able to retire and never work again. They could invest the capital and live on the income from their investments.

10. While the business in each case appeared to grow from nothing, actually there was generally a period of work without income.

In the case of the insurance agency it took about twelve months for the first income to arrive. During those twelve months contacts were made with financial institutions and dealers by means of extensive mailings and trips by automobile. This preparatory work incurred expenses at a time when the business was not earning an income.

The mortality of new businesses is very high, and most fail because there is not enough capital in the business to keep it going until money begins to come in. For the owners of most of the businesses described above, the main expenditures were for mailings, telephones, and travel, besides paying the grocery bills until the business began to earn.

11. In probably every case the amount of work and dedication involved in establishing the business was very great.

In the organization of any new business the necessary amount of time on the job is often staggering, and the overtime can continue for years until the business is on its feet. Many businesses fail simply because not enough time and attention are given to them by their owners.

The amount of emotional strain is also very great, and crises are usual for years in some cases. During the period that the business faces recurrent crises there is often no compensation to the owners out of profits, since profits are nonexistent or very limited.

12. In each of the above businesses the idea was good. If the underlying idea is sound, the business has a chance of big success. Otherwise its future is very doubtful.

13. The buyer of each of these businesses believed in the idea and the organization enough to buy it for a substantial sum of money.

Buying a business with little cash

Substantial sums of money are not always needed to purchase an already established business. It is not at all unusual to be able to buy a going business with a small cash down payment. The business that can be bought for little cash can even be a profitable business, sometimes a highly profitable one. The cash required to close the deal can be little by anybody's standards.

Several years ago this writer purchased a business for

what at the time for him was a considerable amount of cash. The business was a mobile home sales lot at a strategic location in Miami—Seventy-ninth Street near the Hialeah Park racetrack. Sales records showed that the business was profitable.

The purchase price of $55,000 bought the new mobile homes at their factory selling prices plus their transportation to Miami and the used mobile homes at their trade-in allowances.

A new truck and leasehold improvements—landscaping, a large shed, an office, and a large sign, all of which cost about $15,000 when new—were included in the sale at no extra cost.

As soon as the deal was closed, this writer put in another $17,000, making a total cash investment of $72,000, to include mobile homes from several manufacturers, as the sales lot had been the exclusive dealer of just one manufacturer.

A major purpose in buying the sales lot was to provide an interest for two retiring family members while they lived in the pleasant climate of Miami. This plan did not work out, due to a death in the family, and this writer was in the unwanted position of trying to supervise the Miami business from a distance of 1,200 miles.

The operation of a mobile home sales lot at the time did not require a great deal of expertise or technical knowledge, and some of the most successful mobile home businesses were operated by husband-and-wife teams. One such couple was interested in buying our mobile home lot. They had a small lot but felt ready for a larger operation although they had little cash. The sale of the lot was concluded with a cash down payment from them of $2,315.

Why was a business that had recently cost $72,000 sold for $2,315 cash down? The answer is that this writer was anxious to unload a business for which he no longer had a need and which was not a great profit-maker. Then, too, the buyer seemed to know the business and had a good credit rating. We felt fairly certain that the couple would make enough profit on the sales lot to be able to meet each note as it fell due and pay off the entire balance of the purchase price over a period of a year and a half.

At the end of one year of management by the buyer, the sales lot was operating at a good profit and all the notes due had been paid off—six months before the deadline.

From the point of view of the buyer, the business purchased for $2,315 down, including $15,000 worth of leasehold improvements, parts, and equipment, turned out to be a very good investment as well as a means of earning a livelihood.

It is possible to purchase a business with only a small down payment, or even without any down payment, when one or more of the following circumstances exist:

1. It appears to the sellers that the prospective buyer will be able to operate the business at a profit and thus meet the required periodic payments. It may be arranged that payments are made out of profits only, so that if there are no profits no payments are required.

2. The buyer's credit is good and it can be assumed that the required payments will be made.

3. The seller may be operating at a loss and thus may be willing to sell on almost any terms, with the assumption that the buyer can turn the loss into a profit.

4. The seller may be old or infirm or both and just want to get out of the business.

5. The business may have to be sold in order to settle an estate. In this circumstance there may be very little bargaining on the part of the executors who simply want to close out the estate.

6. The seller may want to sell on the time-payment plan in order to minimize his tax liability by turning what would otherwise be ordinary income into a capital gain.

Borrowing for business

The main source of funds for the vast majority of new businesses is the savings of those who establish the businesses. In a study made by the U.S. Department of Commerce it was found that two-thirds of the total investment in new businesses in the wholesale and retail fields came from the savings of the new operators and perhaps family, friends, and associates. Even enterprises with assets of over $100,000 were mostly funded from savings. Still, almost no business enterprise, whether large or small, operates without credit in some form.

The two great financial means of operating businesses are risk or equity capital on the one hand and borrowing on the other. To understand borrowing as a means of building capital, it is important to know why and under what conditions a person will lend funds.

A loan is an obligation on the part of the borrower to repay a given sum at a certain time. This obligation can be enforced against the borrower by legal means if necessary. There is a fixed rate of return to the lender. The importance of this aspect of borrowing cannot be overemphasized. The lender can count on a stable income from loans made, and the interest rate is usually very much higher than the dividend rate on stocks. Although there is no appreciation of the loan's principal, the lender considers the fixed rate of return more important than capital appreciation.

The basic reason one borrows for business purposes is to make a profit on the borrowed money. The borrower must be able to pay the required interest and at the same time secure a higher rate of return on the borrowed money in order to make a profit.

Loans can be obtained from several sources. It is possible to receive relatively small unsecured loans from banks and other credit institutions simply on the basis of the fact that the borrower is a stable individual with a good credit rating and a continuing source of income.

The biggest source of funds, from a borrowing point of view, is residential mortgages. There are few home-owners who have not at one time or another taken out a mortgage in order to purchase a home. It is also possible to mortgage one's home in order to obtain funds for a legitimate business purpose if the home is free of a mort-gage. And it is possible to increase one's mortgage at a bank or savings and loan association to secure funds for a business enterprise.

One of the most successful financiers in the country began his career by acquiring mortgages on properties. He started out by lending, say, $2,000 to a property own-er and obtaining a mortgage on the borrower's home. Then he deposited $10,000 in a bank. At about the same time that he made the deposit he took his $2,000 mort-gage to the bank and borrowed 75 percent of the mort-gage's value.

In the course of a year he may have taken three such mortgages to the bank in order to borrow 75 percent on them. There was no risk to the bank since he had more money in the bank ($10,000) than the total of his borrow-ings against his mortgages. Any bank would like to make such risk-free loans all the time.

But this man was building up to something. He let the bank hold his mortgages and watch how the debtors paid. In this way the bank became more confident about the mortgages as well as about his business ability.

At the end of a year this man proposed to borrow more against the mortgages than the $10,000 he had on deposit in the bank. By this time the bank had enough experi-ence with the mortgages and with him to trust the credit of both.

Now he would begin to profit. The mortgages bore a high rate of interest—much above the 6 percent he had to pay the bank on loans at the time. Over a period of years he developed the following pattern of financing his mortgages with banks:

He took a $10,000 mortgage to the bank and borrowed 75 percent of it—$7,500. With this money he bought another mortgage for $7,500. This $7,500 mortgage he took to the bank and borrowed 75 percent of it—$5,625—and with this sum he bought still another mortgage. He extended this process as far as possible, each time receiving less money from the bank and each time reinvesting these lesser sums in more mortgages.

To summarize, his initial $10,000 enabled him to buy about $40,000 worth of mortgages. His capital was, in effect, multiplied by four.

If this mortgage lender had placed his $10,000 in a mortgage at 12 percent interest—his rate at the time—his annual income would have been $1,200. But he borrowed an additional $30,000 in this pyramiding operation and thus ran his capital up to $40,000. He paid 6 percent interest on his $30,000 of borrowings and obtained 12 percent interest on it. His net profit was thus 6 percent on $30,000—$1,800 per year. This $1,800 added to the $1,200 on his own $10,000 added up to $3,000—a 30 percent return on his $10,000.

This lender eventually had a vast amount of money invested in this way, and he operated the entire business out of a small office in the basement of his home. He employed an accountant for a few hours each week and hired a secretary only when he had some letters to write, so his overhead was small. His annual income from this operation ran well into six figures.

The main reason he made such a success of this business was his ability to acquire good mortgages, not those that were unsound and defaulted.

Apart from his pyramiding operation, this financier became wealthy by purchasing just two properties. Some years ago he wanted to buy two apartment houses on New York City's West Side. The buildings were old and their rents were controlled, so they did not return much when compared with newer apartment houses.

Borrowing on Mortgages
For Non-Real-Estate Purposes

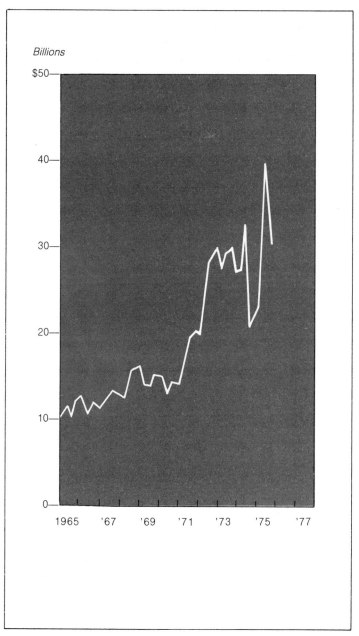

Source: The Conference Board

The financier was able to secure first mortgages on the two buildings at 6 percent interest, but when he added up the amount that could be obtained from the bank on first mortgages plus what he had in the bank, the total fell far short of the $2 million purchase price. So he obtained a second mortgage, on which he had to pay 18 percent per year—three times the interest rate of the first mortgage.

At the end of about ten years his entire investment in the two buildings was free of any indebtedness, the mortgages having been paid off with money from the rents received from the tenants of the buildings.

Theoretically, the investor now owned two buildings worth $2 million. In the ten-year period, however, real estate values in New York City had risen considerably. Instead of being worth $2 million the buildings were worth $8 million. In this way an investment of virtually nothing (because of a combination of first and second mortgages) turned into $8 million in about ten years.

Using "other people's money"

"Other people's money," or "O.P.M.," is a common term in the field of finance. It means employing the funds of others in one's business for the purpose of making a profit on those funds.

It is not often possible to make a profit on other people's money unless one provides a good return to the suppliers of the money. The board of directors or the business entrepreneur hopes to make more money on O.P.M. than that money costs.

Several years ago a financial specialist who knew loans and mortgages well organized a business—a rather unusual one at that time. It was a partnership with three general partners and fifty limited partners. General partners run a business and are unlimited as to their liability for debts. Limited partners usually are responsible for debts only to the extent of their investment.

The main general partner was the finance man who organized the business. The two other general partners were his brother-in-law and a business associate. Each of these three contributed $10,000 to the partnership and the fifty limited partners contributed a total of $1,028,000—making $1,058,000 in capital. Then more people wanted to get into the partnership, so the total capital was increased to $1,108,000.

The purpose of the partnership was to make business loans at high interest rates. Bank funds were available to the partners because the business idea was sound and because the partnership's capital amply protected the banks from losses on any loans that went bad.

In its first three months of operation the partnership earned $51,000. This return represented 4.6 percent on the capital invested for one-quarter of a year. On the basis of a full year of operation, profits would be four times this or 18.4 percent. Few business organizations of any kind can boast of such progress in so short a time.

The partners received $23,000 in disbursements for the first three months. By the end of the next three months, the operation was fully under way. Profits amounted to $54,000, and this sum was distributed to the partners. The return on capital was at an annual rate of 17 percent. In the next quarter profits were $58,000. The profits jumped to $79,000 in the following quarter. For the next quarter of the year, profits were $78,000. The profit for the calendar year was $269,000.

From the beginning, more people wanted to get into the business as limited partners than could be accommodated. The company regularly paid 1 percent per month—12 percent per year—to the limited partners.

From the point of view of the three general partners, earnings were very satisfactory. Returns on capital earnings were credited to the three general partners who had contributed $10,000 each.

By the end of the following year, capital had been in-

Organizational Setups
Of U.S. Businesses

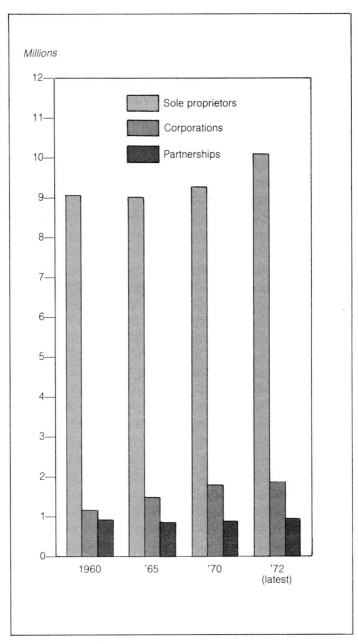

Millions

- Sole proprietors
- Corporations
- Partnerships

1960 '65 '70 '72 (latest)

Source: Internal Revenue Service

creased to $2,365,000. Earnings for the year were $346,000. Of this sum, the three general partners got one-fourth, or $86,500 ($28,833 each). At that time each of the general partners could have sold his investment of $10,000 for at least $100,000.

There were several reasons for the success of this business:

1. The organizers, particularly the main general partner, knew where to get good business right away. There was thus an immediate source of income for the partnership.

2. The organizers had the ability to assess each risk well and rapidly before they placed the partnership's funds.

3. They knew how to operate the business and how to collect.

4. They had some bank connections and some reputation with banks for successfully handling money.

5. The general partners had enough of a reputation for successfully operating a business to attract limited partners.

6. The general partners had something very substantial to offer the limited partners—12 percent a year as a return on their capital.

7. The organization was a partnership so there was no corporation tax. Earnings were taxed only to the individual partners receiving distributions of earnings.

8. The organizers were well able to judge earnings in advance of starting operations, unlike most organizers of new businesses. The limited partners were satisfied with a 12 percent annual return and were not particularly concerned about how much of the earnings went to the general partners.

Here is another way O.P.M. is used:
Right now in various parts of the country there are

thriving businesses in the brokerage of loans and mortgages. This type of business is even thriving in New York City despite the fact that New York real estate took a terrible tumble during the last four years. This brokerage business is so successful because there is almost always a demand for funds that banks cannot supply. The sum involved may be too large for the banks in view of the lack of size or strength of the property against which the loan must be made. Or the loan applicant may be in an area not served by many banks. Or the type of loan may not be approved by banks. Second mortgages are not placed by banks, and this is one area in which loan brokers operate in great numbers and with large sums of money.

Very often banks or savings and loan associations will supply money for construction loans for commercial buildings or groups of homes being erected by builders. Sometimes the money supplied for construction proves to be too little to complete the buildings. The obvious thing for the builder to do is to ask the bank for more money. At that point, however, the bank may not want to risk any further funds. The builder or owner of the uncompleted property may then have to go to other sources.

This was the experience of the owner-builder of a catering establishment in New York who needed an additional $100,000 to complete his building. The answer was to borrow $100,000 from a group of people, each of whom was willing to risk money for a period of two years in return for a high rate of interest. The borrower felt that in two years his business would be operating profitably and he would be able to repay the $100,000 with interest. For the loan of $100,000 he agreed to pay back $120,000 at the end of two years, which amounts to a return of 10 percent per year. There were four participants in this loan, each lending $25,000. Each received a 10 percent annual return on his money. In addition, the loan was repaid ahead of schedule because this catering business was an enormous success.

A loan broker seeks out such needs for money by those willing to pay high interest rates. The rates are high because the suppliers of the money must take a position inferior to that of the bank. In case of default and foreclosure the bank is paid off first, and there may be little or nothing to repay the suppliers of the supplementary funds.

It is entirely usual for the broker to be paid for his services in finding such special situations for loans, putting the lending group together, handling the legal and paper work, and collecting the repayments due.

To simplify a case, let us assume that a builder requires $100,000 for one year. The loan broker says that the money can be supplied by a group which the broker will get together; and the builder at the end of one year must pay back $115,000, representing a 15 percent return to the lenders. However, when the $115,000 is repaid, the loan broker keeps $5,000 for himself. Thus $10,000 goes to the suppliers of the money, yielding them 10 percent on their investment.

If the loan broker makes ten such deals in a year (and many of them make more than ten deals a year), he receives $50,000. The broker's earnings come from "other people's money." He may put into the loan some of his own funds. If he puts little or none of his own money into each loan, his risk of loss is of course minimal or nonexistent.

Such brokerage activities can extend to all sorts of business deals—loans to complete construction of houses or commercial structures, second mortgages which homeowners want for one reason or another, land purchases, building purchases, and commercial loans of all kinds.

Getty's views on wealth-building

If you are considering using your savings or O.P.M. to start a new business or to purchase an existing one, you may wish to bear in mind the following views of J. Paul

Getty on the subject of building wealth. It was the example of "how Paul Getty did it" that spurred this writer to begin building capital. Getty said:

"1. The only way to make a great deal of money is in *one's own business*. One should have a basic knowledge of the business before going into it and he should acquire an extremely thorough knowledge of it as rapidly as possible as he goes along.

"2. The businessman must save not only in his business enterprise but in his personal life in order to build. Only after he has 'made it' can he feel free to spend it.

"3. The businessman must be patient, let the business grow naturally and not 'force it' in order to get rich quick.

"4. The businessman must be willing to take risks with his own as well as with borrowed money, remembering that he must one day pay back the borrowed money. Only by taking a risk can he hope to become wealthy.

"5. The businessman must not only learn to live with tension; he must seek tension so that he is always alert to new opportunities and new ways of operating his business better.

"6. The businessman should concentrate on building wealth as a by-product of making more and better things more cheaply for more people. Only by doing for someone else can he expect to secure something in return.

"7. Paradoxically enough, the man who is too interested in money may not make it. He should concentrate on building his business and not spend too much time 'counting his gold' until he has it in the bank."

One more principle might be added to Paul Getty's guide to wealth-building, although perhaps his last point implies it and leads into it. At some point the business owner who wants to build wealth should attempt to realize some cash. This point should come at the top of the prosperity cycle of the business. Usually the top of the cycle for a business is the top of the cycle for the industry in which the business operates.

At the peak of this cycle the business owner should either (1) liquidate in part, probably by selling a portion of the business, or (2) sell out, or (3) refrain from rapid expansion and try to get some cash out of the business in dividends, or (4) float some type of security to preserve the capital needed in the business while retaining control of the business.

Securities and Exchange Commission records are full of descriptions of capital issues that resulted in bonanzas for the owners or part-owners of corporations.

A clothing manufacturer, for example, sought permission to issue 110,000 shares of stock at $3.50 per share. The net proceeds of this underwriting after expenses were to be $313,500. At that time the company had 150,000 shares of stock outstanding, and one-third of that stock was owned by the president, one-third by the vice-president, and one-third by the treasurer.

The sale of the new stock at $3.50 per share was to increase the book value of the stock outstanding from 54 cents to $1.52 per share, with a resulting dilution of $1.98 per share in the book equity of the stock purchased by the public. In other words, the 150,000 shares outstanding before the proposed new financing were represented by net assets, or net worth, of 54 cents a share—$81,000.

If 110,000 shares and $313,500 were added by the company, the result would be 260,000 shares and $394,500. Dividing the money by the number of shares would provide the net book value per share—$1.52.

The original stockholders who owned 150,000 shares, represented by $81,000 or 54 cents per share, then would have 150,000 shares represented by $1.52 per share— $228,000. They would make a profit on the deal of $228,000 minus $81,000, or $147,000.

This is one way that the owner of a business can acquire

a sizable amount of money with little or no original investment.

Whatever method is chosen, the goal should be to get
some cash into the hands of the business owner, who can
either set aside the money as a cushion or diversify into
other areas of investment to continue building wealth.

CHAPTER 8

Putting
Your
Capital
to Work

When one depends on capital to provide a living year in and year out, it can be a matter of investment survival. In the case of many, if not most, people who live by their investments, at times the struggle is grim.

This is why the owner of a fund of wealth usually does not sit around and think, "How can I become wealthier?" but rather, "What can I do today so that six months or a year from now I will not be in a financial crisis?"

Right now those who survived the 1973-75 recession are in the process of recuperating. A very few of the wealthy continued to do well throughout that economic crisis. But most suffered, some tremendously.

What lies ahead is more inflation, and everyone with a fund of wealth, no matter how small, should take action now to protect this fund from being eroded and to make

How U.S. Millionaires
Spread Their Assets

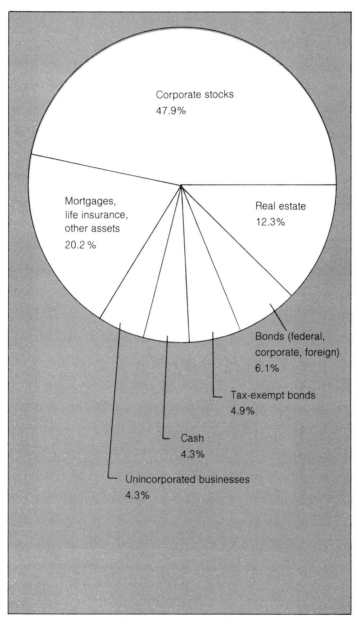

Corporate stocks
47.9%

Mortgages,
life insurance,
other assets
20.2 %

Real estate
12.3%

Bonds (federal,
corporate, foreign)
6.1%

Tax-exempt bonds
4.9%

Cash
4.3%

Unincorporated businesses
4.3%

Sources: U.S. Department of the Treasury, Federal Reserve Board

assets earn as much as possible in this inflationary era.

Investing in stocks

Anyone who studies the publication *Statistics of Income*, issued periodically by the Internal Revenue Service, cannot help but come to the conclusion that the principal way to become wealthy in the United States is to invest in the stock market. At least the statistics show that the stock market is the main source of capital gains for Americans.

While the stock market is the main means of achieving capital gains it is also probably the main cause of capital losses for a vast number of people. The stock market is like a giant roulette wheel. Some players win and some lose, and among the winners are some who win enormous sums of money.

In addition to offering an opportunity to experience capital gains, the stock market is a means of securing a periodic return on one's capital.

The main risk of the stock market, of course, is that stocks decline at times. One can minimize this risk by selling before the stock goes down very far. Or one can place a stop order below the market so that a dropping market triggers the stop order and the owner of the stock is automatically sold out of the stock.

But things do not seem to work this way. Investors are reluctant to sell on a declining market. They may rationalize that they are in for the long pull, not for quick profits, and that they do not care what happens short of, say, five or ten years.

The answer is that it would have been better to sell at 1,000 in 1972 than to have waited until late 1974 when the Dow Jones industrial average hit 578. One could have sold out $10,000 worth of stock and then bought it all back for $5,780. The "five or ten years investment theory" also applies to stocks bought in 1929 or earlier and carried through 1932.

Another rationalization about a declining market is at times certain to result in losses. This reasoning is not to sell on a declining market but to hold on to the stock since "the market is bound to go up again some time." It will go up, but first it may go down for a long time and a great amount.

Thus the downside risk of the stock market is very great. Even the most prestigious financial institutions handling the portfolios of investors have been known to stand by and watch a client's stocks go down the drain. Recently one investor who had entrusted his portfolio and its management to a large and highly regarded New York bank visited the bank to see what had happened to his portfolio of $15 million. It had declined, under the management of this bank, to $10 million.

The same bank also handled his wife's portfolio of over $2 million. This had declined to less than $1 million.

This couple asked for checks representing their entire investment portfolio, thanked the bank very much for its management of their funds, and went home with what was left of their money. Few financial institutions managing investment portfolios for individuals will ever say, "We think the market is going into a decline, so we sold all of your stocks, and the money is all there in cash waiting for you to pick it up or waiting until the market hits bottom and turns up."

Building wealth with stocks

The technique of picking a winner in the stock market is very much like that of picking an artist whose paintings are selling for a few hundred dollars now but will one day sell for thousands or even hundreds of thousands of dollars. Picking a potential winner early in the game, before prices have risen, is a most difficult one.

Some years ago James Couzens, who later became a U.S. senator, bought twenty-five shares of stock in a new corporation for $2,500, paying $100 a share. He paid

$1,000 in cash and gave four-month notes for the remaining $1,500. Subsequently he paid off the notes and owned the stock free and clear. He gave one share of the stock to his sister. His net investment then became $2,400.

The new corporation prospered, and four years later Couzens purchased an additional fifty shares of the stock plus thirty-one shares of the company's Canadian affiliate for a total of $25,000, so that the average price per share of the second stock purchase was over three times what the original shares had cost him.

Four months later he bought another thirty-five shares of the stock for $17,500, an average price of $500 per share. Now James Couzens had 109 shares of the company plus thirty-one shares of its Canadian affiliate.

One year later the company issued a stock dividend of 1,900 percent, which gave Couzens 2,071 shares. These shares plus his 109 shares added up to 2,180 shares. He had invested a total of $44,900 in the stock.

Eleven years later Couzens sold his 2,180 shares of stock back to the corporation for $29,308,857.90. Shortly before he sold the stock back to the corporation—the Ford Motor Company—he received a cash dividend of $2,101,017.07 plus interest of $167,505.74.

This can be described as a prime example of building wealth through the purchase of stock.

Those who seek to build wealth through investing in stocks should remember that, in general, wealth can be created through stock ownership in only two ways: (1) appreciation in the price of the stock, and (2) dividends, which arise out of earnings.

To assess the stock market as a source of wealth we might use the basic criteria for investing in any business. Two general questions must be answered before money is put into a new business venture: (1) Is the investment sound in that dollars invested will be preserved, and (2) what will the money invested in this venture earn?

The preservation of capital is basic and need not be

explained further. As for earnings, they alone must provide a return on the money invested as well as growth in the assets of the company and its net worth so that what the investors put into the company will grow.

It must be remembered that we are looking at the entire stock market as a means of building wealth. We are not trying to select individual stocks for their growth potential or because we think they are underpriced. For many years it has been the belief of a major proportion of American investors that wealth could be built in the stock market as a whole, provided particular stocks were selected with some degree of intelligence. Let us see what can be expected from the stock market over a period of investing for several years, without trying to pick winners by hindsight.

First, let us find out what one can expect from the stock market as regards capital appreciation. In other words, if one put $100 or $1,000 or $1 million into the stock market, what can be reasonably expected by way of appreciation of this sum, based on the past performance of the market? We might use a reasonable investment period to make this assessment, say from the start of the 1960s to the present. We might also use a broad average of many stocks, such as Standard and Poor's average of 500 stocks or Standard and Poor's industrial average. The base period of these is 1941-43, but any base period can be used as a benchmark.

Looking at the table on page 179 we find that if a person in 1961 invested $68.27 in a "composite" of the stock market this sum as of late 1976 would have grown to $107.46. The investment increased 60 percent in a span of fifteen years—about 4 percent per year. The industrial company stocks did a little better. Had one sold them out in 1972, the increase would have been even higher—about 74 percent in eleven years, almost 7 percent per year.

Judging by this table the stock market, overall, does not

Security Price Index Record
(Standard and Poor's)

	500 Stocks	425 Industrials
1961	68.27	69.99
1962	62.38	65.54
1963	69.87	73.39
1964	81.37	86.19
1965	88.17	93.48
1966	85.26	91.08
1967	91.93	99.18
1968	98.69	107.50
1969	97.84	107.20
1970	83.22	91.20
1971	98.29	108.40
1972	109.20	121.80
1973	107.40	120.50
1974	82.85	92.91
1975	86.16	96.56
1976	107.46	116.33
Early 1977	105.20	116.83

appear to be an outstanding way to build capital. If we change the figures in the stock index to dollars we have, let us say, $6,827 instead of 68.27 in 1961. For early 1977 the figure might well be $10,520 instead of 105.20. The $6,827 invested in 1961 becomes $10,520 in 1977. If we take the most favorable year in the table, 1972, the capital shows a theoretical growth from $6,827 to $10,920 eleven years later. The growth is not spectacular.

Spectacular growth might, however, be achieved by investing in the stock market cyclically. The market moves cyclically—from low to high to low to high—mainly as a parallel to prosperity and recession, but on occasion independently of the underlying national economy.

Using the highs and lows from the index of industrial stocks prepared by Standard and Poor's, the cyclical movement becomes apparent for the period from 1961 to 1977:

**Standard and Poor's Industrials
On Selected Dates**

December 1961	75.81
October 1962	58.66
January 1966	99.56
October 1966	82.01
December 1968	116.00
June 1970	82.96
January 1973	132.60
December 1974	74.80
November 1975	100.90
January 1977	116.83

When we study the highs and the lows which follow one another fairly regularly throughout history, and very likely will follow one another in the future as they have in the past, it seems possible to invest on a cyclical basis without a great degree of loss at any point in the cycle. It should, however, be emphasized that it is impossible to buy into the market at its low point and sell at its high. The low point must be watched for signs of a sustained upward movement. Similarly, one must watch for a movement downward of some duration before coming to the conclusion that we are in a bear market. Turns of the market can be determined, but not the exact turning points.

From the above table, it appears that the market declined over 22 percent from December 1961 to October 1962. If a person bought stock in October 1962, by January 1966 the investment would have increased by 70 percent in a little over three years. Before 1966 was over, however, the level of the market declined 18 percent. In

Dividends and Earnings
In Relation to Stock Price
(Standard and Poor's Corporate Series)

	Common Dividend to Price Ratio	Earnings to Price Ratio
1970	3.83	6.46
1971	3.14	5.41
1972	2.84	5.50
1973	3.06	7.12
1974	4.47	11.60
1975	4.31	9.03
1976	4.05	11.10

the next two years, to the peak of December 1968, the rise was 41 percent, over 20 percent per year. In the next year and a half, to June 1970, all of the increase had been erased.

This was followed by a massive rise, which lifted the average of the market from 82.96 to 132.6—60 percent— in just two and a half years. Then a disastrous decline set in, which carried the average to its low point in December 1974. The stocks, on the average, lost 44 percent of their value. At that point, a rise began which brought the average to 116.83 by the beginning of 1977—a rise of 56 percent.

Cyclical investing most certainly can build wealth.

Using stocks for reasonable returns

The stock market as a wealth-builder is one thing. The stock market as a means of making assets earn a good rate of return over a period of years is another. Actually, the stock market can fairly well be counted on to provide a

Dow Jones Industrial Average, Earnings, and Dividends

	Dow Jones Average	Annual Earnings	Dividends
March 1963	$ 682	$ 37.35	--
End 1963	763	41.21	$23.41
End 1964	874	46.43	31.24
End 1965	969	53.67	28.61
End 1966	785	57.68	31.89
End 1967	905	53.87	30.19
End 1968	944	57.89	31.34
End 1969	800	57.02	33.90
End 1970	839	51.02	31.53
End 1971	890	55.09	30.86
End 1972	1,020	67.11	32.27
End 1973	850	86.17	35.33
End 1974	616	99.04	37.72
End 1975	852	75.66	37.46
End 1976	1,004	95.81	41.40

reasonable annual return on money invested, with some appreciation as assets and earnings of the underlying companies continue to grow, as the table on page 181 shows.

A highly important and extremely positive fact in connection with the stock market is the growth of earnings in the last several years. To indicate the significance of this growth to the investor we might turn to the Dow Jones industrial average of thirty selected large companies,

Dow Jones Industrials Price
In Relation to Earnings and Dividends

	Price-Earnings Ratio	Price-Dividends Ratio
March 1963	18.3	--
End 1963	18.5	32
End 1964	18.8	28
End 1965	18.1	33
End 1966	13.6	25
End 1967	16.8	30
End 1968	16.3	30
End 1969	14.0	23
End 1970	16.4	27
End 1971	16.2	29
End 1972	15.2	31
End 1973	9.9	24
End 1974	6.2	16
End 1975	11.3	23
End 1976	10.5	24

shown in the table at the top of page 182. Whether representative of the entire stock market or not, this is the most used and most quoted of all stock averages.

From 1963 through 1976 the Dow Jones industrial average has been characterized by more of an up-and-down movement than by growth. If we relate the figure in 1976 to the earliest in the table—March 1963—we find a growth of about 47 percent in thirteen years—about 3.6 percent per year.

Earnings, on the other hand, have shown not only a steady, but a substantial, growth from 37.35 to 95.81—

over 155 percent in the period, or about 12 percent per year. Dividends rose 76 percent in the period, about 6 percent a year.

At the top of page 183 is a table showing the same type of information, but as a reciprocal—how many times annual earnings and annual dividends these stocks were selling for.

The period covered in these two tables was not a spectacular one for the stock market. Stock prices did not rise as they did after World War II and particularly in the 1950s. Neither did earnings or dividends rise enormously. Still, when analyzed objectively, the stock market turned in a good performance in this period for anyone who simply invested money for reasonable growth and for adequate, increasing return on the investment.

The person who invested in 1963 at 763 saw the investment rise to 1,004 at the end of 1976 while dividends rose from 23.41 to 41.40. In this period the investment rose by about 32 percent and the dividend yield on it rose to 5.4 percent. The earnings amounted to 12½ percent on the original investment.

Advantages of investing in stocks

The major reasons why the stock market is an important and popular medium for investors are as follows:

1. Funds are instantly available. To be able to get your money out when needed on virtually a day's notice is a big advantage. There is almost no other high-yield or high-potential capital gain investment that offers the liquidity of the stock market.

2. There is little possibility that one will be caught in a default. In real estate, defaults seemed to be the rule rather than the exception in the period 1973-76. Almost all large portfolios of loans and mortgages experience losses, some of the magnitude of the Real Estate Investment Trusts that have suffered huge losses. Even in the

bond market, defaults on listed bonds are not very common. Since financial reports are periodically available,
one can often see trouble coming and get out of a stock or
a bond before trouble actually develops. Even the so-
called junk bonds result in relatively few defaults.

3. There is no possibility of being caught in a currency
devaluation. In the recent drop of the Mexican peso,
creditors' losses were enormous, even on loans extended
to the most credit-worthy firms in the world that were
denominated in pesos instead of in dollars, Swiss francs,
German marks, or other hard currencies. Even a devaluation of the dollar does not hurt the person who lives and
spends in the United States.

4. Price increases result in capital gains, which are in
the "tax-preferred" category, being taxed at a rate of up
to 25 percent if the gain is $50,000 or less and 35 percent
if the gain is greater than $50,000. Ordinary income is
taxed at rates of up to 70 percent. There is also the alternative of adding half of the capital gain to ordinary income and applying the regular tax rate to it—a process
that results in a tax rate of only one-half of the usual rate.

5. The investment is usually in the larger corporations
of the country. As a general rule, the larger the corporation the less likely is it to go into bankruptcy. A large
corporation can lose money for years and still not default,
remaining credit-worthy.

6. To the investor in stocks, corporate dishonesty is not
as important as it is in other types of investments that
offer the prospect of high yields. Any bank credit officer
or any finance company official knows of many losses that
have resulted from the dishonesty of borrowers. Such
losses by creditors are far from unusual. If a corporation's
officials are dishonest, this does not so easily have an ad-
verse effect on the price of the stock or the solvency of
the firm.

7. Overall, the return on stocks is good. The decade of
the 1950s was better than now, and the "go-go" years of

the 1960s produced some fantastic capital gains. Still, the 1970s, while by no means good every year so far, have shown a generally satisfactory combination of appreciation and dividends, provided one did not buy in early 1966, when the Dow Jones industrial average stood at over 1,000, and sell in late 1974, when it stood at 578!

Investing for high returns

The stock market is essentially an equity type of investment. True, stocks pay dividends, but they are generally not high, so that the owner of the stocks looks to appreciation in price and thus in the value of the investment portfolio.

For the sophisticated investor who is willing to devote some time systematically to locating investment and deposit opportunities and investigating them thoroughly, there is the possibility of high returns.

Fixed-return investments, or fixed-dollar investments, as they are also called, depend for their attractiveness on a high periodic return, often in the form of interest. This return is frequently in excess of 10 percent per annum, sometimes 12 percent per annum and higher. Mortgages of a specialized nature are now returning in many cases more than 15 percent per annum. In foreign markets a rate of up to 20 percent has been available recently.

In these investments there is a credit risk. You may get a return on your money, but the question is, "Will you get a return *of* your money?" Theoretically, the higher the rate of return the riskier is the investment and the less likely it is to be repaid. But for those willing to take the risk it is possible to make assets earn very well indeed.

In the summer of 1971, a prime opportunity opened up for making satisfactory bank deposits. The opportunity was in Brazil. Leading banks in that country were paying 12 percent per annum for deposits, and the term of the deposit was flexible—either long or short. The government of Brazil guaranteed the availability of foreign exchange, so that at the end of the term the deposits could be converted to the currencies of other countries.

At that time the dollar was in a weakened condition. Thus, in 1971 this investor placed $101,030 on deposit in one major Brazilian bank. In another, he placed $41,143. In a third bank, he placed $17,119. Each bank was flexible as to how much it was willing to take on deposit. This depositor denominated the first two deposits in Swiss francs and the third in German marks. The banks were willing to pay in U.S. dollars, Swiss francs, or German marks, or even other currencies, according to the wishes of the depositor.

In all, this depositor had $159,292 in three major Brazilian banks—at 12 percent interest per annum. These time deposits were payable in late 1973.

In late 1971 the dollar was in effect devalued, and formally devalued a few months later by about 8 percent. The second devaluation of the dollar—by 10 percent— took place in February 1973.

The money was placed on deposit in Brazil in 1971 at a rate of $.2853 for the German mark and $.2450 for the Swiss franc. By the time of the second devaluation of the dollar, the Swiss franc stood at $.29326 and the German mark at $.33273. After the second devaluation of the dollar, the German mark and the Swiss franc rose even more. In just two months, between May 4 and July 5, 1973, the German mark rose 24 percent and the Swiss franc rose 18 percent. The Swiss franc then stood at $.3690 and the German mark at $.4410.

At that point this depositor decided to buy forward dollars at the best rate he could get when his deposits became due and payable. In other words, he would be guaranteed a particular rate, regardless of whether the dollar rose or the Swiss franc and the German mark fell. His forward rates were $.3550 for the Swiss franc and $.4230 for the German mark. Now he did not have to worry about rates of conversion back into dollars.

His $159,292 had now grown to $273,480. In addition, he had received $2,912.59 in periodic interest on the German mark notes. The Brazilian government had collected $14,954 in income taxes on the deposits, but this was added to the $273,480, not subtracted from it. In a sense, the gain plus the interest of $2,912.59 were tax-free, as the $14,954 could be used by the income recipient to pay his U.S. income taxes. If, for instance, the bottom line of his income tax return showed a tax due on all of his income from every source of, say, $60,000, he could pay $14,954 of it with his "Brazilian tax credit." The total amount returned to this depositor, with the tax credit added, was $291,346. This was 83 percent more than he had placed on deposit a little over two years earlier, representing a return of 41½ percent per year!

The tax was computed for U.S. income tax purposes in two ways. The 12 percent annual return on the deposits was taxed at ordinary income tax rates; but the rest was a profit which arose through a combination of devaluation of the dollar and revaluation upward of the Swiss franc and the German mark. This was a capital gain and was taxed at essentially half the rate of ordinary income.

Had the funds not been returned to the United States, there would have been no capital gain and no capital gains tax at all on the appreciation—only a tax on the 12 percent interest payable by the banks in Brazil. Thus, more appreciation on the further rise of the Swiss franc and the German mark might have been realized. Still, there were other deposits and loans to make which turned out to be better than the further appreciation of these two currencies after 1973.

High-rate deposits, high-rate loans, and other high-rate investments are often risky. In general, the higher the rate the greater the risk, the high rate being the means of securing funds for less certain investments. From the investor's point of view the rate of return may justify taking the risk. The professional investor may feel also that a high rate of return over a period of years makes an occasional loss acceptable.

An investor who had placed money in Mexico for, say, fifteen years and had received a 12 percent average annual rate of return might have been able to weather the 1976 devaluations of the peso which amounted to about 40 percent. In the three years prior to the devaluation (technically called a float) it was possible to secure returns of up to 20 percent per annum from prime borrowers. A total return over the three-year period of about 60 percent or more was entirely possible. The effect of the devaluation would have been eased considerably. It was also possible, although at times at high cost, to purchase futures contracts to insure against a devaluation.

Let us now take a look at some of the high-rate investment opportunities that exist today.

High-yield bonds

In 1976 it was possible to purchase relatively secure railroad, industrial, and utility bonds that had a current yield of 15 percent or more.

One of the soundest railroads in the country had 4¾ percent and 5 percent bonds outstanding which could have been bought early in 1976 for about 40 or 41, sometimes a little less. The bonds paid 4¾ percent or 5 percent at the time they were issued at or about 100; but when the price dropped to 40, the yield was determined by dividing the rate of 5 percent by the current price of 40—to yield about 12½ percent. One railroad in 1974, at the time of very high interest rates, issued a 12¼ percent bond and this was selling somewhere near 100 in 1976, so that the yield was 12¼ percent.

Of course the people who bought the 4¾ percent or 5 percent bonds when they sold for 100 are neither happy with the present price nor with the yield, with the bonds now selling in the 40s. Bonds, like all other securities, can go down as well as up. It has been entirely possible to buy

5 percent bonds at 50 to yield 10 percent and then watch them decline to 40, so that a bond that sold for $500 gave an annual return of $50 but lost $100 in capital in the decline from $500 to $400.

On the other hand, 1976 was in general a year of rising bond markets. At the end of 1975 this writer purchased railroad bonds at 41. The interest was 4¾ percent, and it was paid April 1, 1976. In September 1976 the bonds were sold at 48. Thus, the return on the bonds was 4¾ percent interest and an appreciation in price of 7 (48 less 41), making a total return of 11¾, or 28 percent, on the bonds bought at 41.

The long-range objective of this investor, as far as bonds go, is not to make a capital gain and sell out but rather to secure a steady return of about 12 percent year in and year out, which return can be secured if one does not sell high and then try to find another bond to yield as much as the bond did when it was bought at 40 or 41.

On the present market it is not difficult to receive yields of over 10 percent on bonds. They may not be the highest-rated bonds, but in a rising economy, bonds are far safer and defaults are far less likely than in a recession.

Specialized mortgages

Specialized mortgages, including second mortgages, are another area of high returns. Here, over the past three years, capital has run a great deal of risk and losses have been heavy. The principal reasons for losses have been skyrocketing operating expenses. The fourfold increase in petroleum costs instituted by the Organization of Petroleum Exporting Countries has caused the cost of heating to soar. In addition, maintenance costs have risen greatly. So have property taxes. The result has been red operating figures for apartment houses and office buildings, which in many cases have defaulted. A large number of office buildings and apartment houses have not simply gone through foreclosure sales; they have actually been abandoned. In the process, mortgage holders have suffered severely. Some mortgages have been completely wiped out, with 100 percent loss of investment funds.

In this situation, holders of second mortgages have suffered much more than first-mortgage holders. If a building was considered to be worth $1 million and the first mortgage was $800,000, a second mortgage might have been placed on the property for, say, $50,000, making the total of mortgages $850,000. This was fine as long as the building was worth $1 million or even $900,000.

As black figures turned red, and foreclosure sales followed defaults, such a building might have sold for $600,000. Under this set of assumptions, the second mortgage would have been wiped out, as well as $200,000 of the first mortgage ($800,000 invested in the first mortgage less the foreclosure sale price of $600,000). This is by no means an overpessimistic assumption.

To cite just one actual case, a graduate of a lower East Side secondary school in New York rose to own properties worth well over $100 million. A few years ago his annual income after using all of the tax-protection techniques available to him was in excess of $2 million. He was respected throughout the business community, particularly the real estate segment of that community.

Then in 1973 trouble set in for New York real estate. His properties were all heavily mortgaged, and they went into the red. One "small" debt that he owed a real estate investment partnership amounted to $160,000. He paid it down to $130,000 but could not pay any more, and the real estate partnership took legal action against him.

But there have been happier outcomes, such as the experience of one property and mortgage manager in New York. Of thirty-four properties on which he and his associates held first or second mortgages through the recent recession, there were three defaults. One resulted in complete loss of the investment. The second default resulted in assumption of ownership of the entire property

by his group. This property is now in the black and, although he and his associates have not received back their
investment or any part of it, they do own a profitable
investment which is paying off the first mortgage systematically, they being the original investors in the second
mortgage. The third defaulted mortgage is on a large and
very expensive row house in New York's East Eighties
area. This property will probably be sold in a foreclosure
sale and the investment group will almost certainly be
paid in full.

The rest of the thirty-four properties in the investment
portfolio are solid and paying. The record is not perfect,
but it is very good for a high-rate investment in the recent recession, particularly a second-mortgage investment.

One type of relatively safe mortgage investment, yield-
ing high rates at the present time, is the purchase-money
mortgage on dwellings. This type of mortgage is used
when the buyer of a property has insufficient funds for a
down payment. In such a case, the seller may wish to
make a concession to close the deal, and therefore takes a
second mortgage on the property.

It works like this: Jones wants to buy Smith's house for
$50,000. The bank will give a $40,000 first mortgage on
it. Jones has only $5,000 with which to buy the property.
He is $5,000 short. Smith very much wants to sell the
property. He feels that Jones is a good credit risk and will
make the monthly payments. In addition, Smith would
like to have a little money out earning a fairly high rate of
interest. So Smith takes a $5,000 purchase-money mort-
gage on the property. This is a second mortgage and
comes behind the bank's first mortgage of $40,000. Now
Jones has the first mortgage for $40,000, his down pay-
ment of $5,000, and Smith's second mortgage for
$5,000—$50,000 in all.

The bank is paid 8¾ percent interest on its mortgage.
On the second mortgage, Smith gets a slightly higher

rate—9 percent. This may not be enough return for the typical second mortgage, but Smith made money on the sale of the house and 9 percent on his $5,000 second mortgage is at least not bad.

As time goes on, however, Smith wishes he had his money out of the second mortgage in order to invest in another property. The second mortgage has two years to run and he wants the money now. So he sells the $5,000 second mortgage for, say, $4,500. He had to lose $500, but he is out of the mortgage and he has the cash in hand that he wants.

In two years, the second mortgage that Smith sold will pay the buyer $5,000, and each year the new holder of the mortgage will receive 9 percent of $5,000, or $450. The $500 discount on the sale of the $5,000 mortgage amounts to $250 a year. This $250 must be added to the $450 annual interest to determine the actual annual yield on the investment of $4,500. The yearly income amounts to $700; and $700 annual return on $4,500 invested is almost 16 percent per annum.

Jones, the owner of the property, feels no greater strain even though the rate to the buyer of the second mortgage is 16 percent. He makes the same interest payments as before—9 percent per annum on the $5,000 second mortgage. The high yield to the holder of the mortgage is the result of having bought it at a discount.

Purchased second mortgages are at present a means of making assets earn for the investor. There is certainly risk in a second mortgage, but the premium rate may offset the risk to a degree.

The first criterion for any specialized mortgage, including a second mortgage, must be: "Is the property worth much more in the market than the total of its mortgages?" If a single-family palatial home on fifteen acres, with a pond and a waterfall, located in Darien, Connecticut, is the security for a $152,000 first mortgage, the property should be worth more than $152,000 in the market—and the market should be a quick one, not one in which it takes years to sell the property.

The example just given was an actual mortgage application. The mortgagor—the owner of the home—sold his fine house with fifteen acres in 1976. He received $380,000 for it, very much more than enough to cover the mortgage.

Had the owner of this property come to a mortgage investor with the home already mortgaged for $152,000, and asked for a $50,000 second mortgage, the decision to grant the second mortgage might not have been made so quickly as was the decision to lend $152,000 on a first mortgage. The year the first mortgage was examined to see whether it would be renewed was 1974, and that year was anything but good for real estate and mortgages. Perhaps a $50,000 second mortgage would have been granted at that time, perhaps not. The house realized $380,000 in the very active and very high 1976 home market.

The investor in a second mortgage must be able to come up with enough money to pay off the first mortgage in order to protect the second mortgage investment in case the owner of the property defaults. Otherwise, in a foreclosure sale, the property might bring less than the total of the first and second mortgages—$202,000 in this example. In poor times the property might bring less than the first mortgage of $152,000 and the second mortgage might be wiped out. The same principle applies to apartment houses, office buildings, shopping centers, and all other properties.

The second criterion is: "Can the mortgagor meet the payments?" In the case of the above house the owner and mortgagor was a motion picture producer. His income usually ran to huge amounts annually. Still, in poor times he might produce nothing and might operate in the red as well as see his cash dwindle. On the other hand, a corporate executive with an income in six figures or close to it, and with a high pension in prospect, might very well carry such a house with a first mortgage of $152,000 and a second of $50,000.

Mortgage investment organizations

Perhaps the worst experience of any type of financial organization has been that of the Real Estate Investment Trusts (REITs). In the recent recession these professionally run organizations, even those operated by the largest banks in the country, experienced disaster.

The reasons for this disaster are: (1) money came in from investors in an enormous flow after REITs were approved as an investment medium, and too much of this money was placed too rapidly and with too little experience in real estate by the financial institutions doing the investing; (2) the operations were too far-flung, some encompassing the entire country or a large part of it, so that credit evaluation and collections were too difficult; and (3) operating expenses rose too fast and too far.

Still, some of the smaller organizations handled such investments far more skillfully because (1) they were operated by real estate professionals; (2) the investments were made nearer to home and could be evaluated and supervised more easily; and (3) there was less pressure from investment funds flooding in.

One such smaller organization was a partnership in Westport, Connecticut. It was composed of a number of limited partners who had liability only to the extent of their investment and three general partners who ran the operation and assumed unlimited liability. The company invested in first and second mortgages, mostly along the East Coast.

Over a period of years, this partnership returned over 14 percent, and often over 15 percent, annually to the limited partners. Payments were made quarterly to the partners.

In the real estate crisis of the early 1970s that continued to 1976, the company for a time suspended payments of income to the partners and instead paid some of the capital back to them. All the money that formerly would have been used to return 14 percent or 15 percent annually to the partners on their investment went into building a reserve for bad debts. In consequence, the partnership weathered the real estate storm.

The main partner of the organization, a tremendously astute real estate investor, took three additional steps: He paid out partners who very much needed the capital they had in the company; he paid out the banks—with his own funds; and he undertook to straighten out problem mortgages at his own expense.

This example is additional proof of the fact that a successful investment in a mortgage investment company depends upon the guiding spirit of the company. Who is this leader and what is his record of success in the mortgage field? In the case of the partnership in Westport, because of the record of the main partner, there were far more applicants for investing than the company wanted to accept.

Too many novice investors place money in companies totally unknown to them and located perhaps 2,000 miles away, then wonder how it was possible for them to have lost so much money so quickly.

Another firm operating along the same lines as the Westport group, but with a different form of organization, is a specialized finance company in New York. This company invests in the same type of mortgages as the Westport partnership but with a corporate form of organization. The investors buy debentures which pay 15 percent per annum. Theoretically, debentures are better than partnerships as a debenture is a definite obligation to pay. If payment is not made, a debenture holder can bring suit to have the corporation thrown into bankruptcy. Actually, probably no debenture holder would take this course of action and instead would attempt to assess the future of the firm if it got into financial trouble. If the future looked good, the holder of debentures would wait for payment. If the outlook seemed bad, the debenture holder would probably request that the corporation liquidate, and the operators, being reasonable people with long experience in mortgage lending, would likely agree.

Specialized mortgages are risky. On the other hand, they return up to 15 percent and even more, and if they are handled by professional managers who are competent, experienced, and honest, such investments can be profitable with a minimum of risk.

While the real estate investment group or loan and mortgage company may hold millions of dollars worth of receivables, these consist of both small and large individual loans and mortgages. The employee of such a company can very well go into the market and buy a mortgage or make a loan for his or her own account and thus get started up the wealth-building ladder.

One such employee in the course of his work has learned how to appraise loans, how to judge risks, how to collect, and what action to take in case of slow payment or default. He now personally invests about $500 in each risk or loan and has several such loans out at this time, either on his own or as a participant with others. As he saves a portion of his income he invests his savings, and as he invests, his loans and mortgages earn. His income increases and he is able to accumulate more savings to invest in more loans and mortgages. This is an example of "falling into wealth" through associating with wealth-builders and learning wealth-building techniques.

Loans to international companies

Over a period of at least fifteen years, major companies operating internationally have borrowed in the currency of the countries in which they operate. It is normal for an international company to borrow locally, but the banks of many countries have not been in a position to accommodate the credit demands of the multinationals.

Leading international companies have borrowed from banks, finance companies, and individuals wherever there were those willing to lend to them in the currencies of the countries in which they were operating. Even such large and sound companies as General Motors Acceptance Corporation and Nestlé of Switzerland have borrowed internationally for their operations in Mexico and elsewhere. They preferred to borrow in the local currencies and repay in the local currencies, thereby avoiding the risk of having to repay in hard currencies, including the dollar, should a devaluation of the local currency take place.

Generally, such loans have been syndicated. A finance company might make a loan of, say, $1 million and then "sell off" parts of it—$100,000, $50,000, or whatever denominations suited the participants in the loan. The finance company made a profit on this splitting up of the loan, but sometimes only a modest profit. If enough of such syndication business was done, however, the commissions to the finance company could amount to a sizable sum. Theoretically, the finance company could sell out each note or loan completely so that it would have no capital of its own invested and so run no credit risk.

In the years 1973 through 1976, major international companies borrowed for their Latin American operations. These international loans are usually made on the basis of discount, and the discount has run all the way from 12 percent to 17½ percent in the past three years. Let us use as an example a discount rate of 15 percent, which was available before the devaluation of the Mexican peso as well as immediately after the devaluation.

The company operating in Mexico proposed, let us say, to borrow $500,000. The finance company in the United States took the entire note and split it into ten equal parts (as an example only—they might have split it into two parts or fifteen or any number). In this case each part was $50,000.

A $50,000 portion was offered to an investor at 15 percent discount, which means an investment in a one-year note of $50,000 less 15 percent, or $7,500—$42,500.

The investor's actual return is calculated by dividing the interest of $7,500 by the invested capital of $42,500, giving a return of 17.65 percent per annum. In addition, the investor receives a tax credit roughly equal to one or two percentage points and, with limitations, can use this Mexican tax credit to pay U.S. income tax.

The return on these loans made to prime credit risks (and a few near-prime credit risks) is very high; but so is the risk of currency devaluation.

It is unsafe to lend in other than very hard currencies, such as the present U.S. dollars, Swiss francs, and German marks. If an individual lends to a Latin American country at, say, a 12 percent discount for a year and after ten months the country devalues its currency modestly, by perhaps 12 percent, all of the income from the loan is lost. In the present devaluation cycle, 12 percent is a modest figure indeed. Mexico, in several months, devalued its currency about 40 percent, so that all of a year's interest and perhaps another 30 percent of capital would be lost. In the present international market one should stick to a rigid principle of investing either in dollars or in other strong currencies. And remember that even the strongest currencies have been devalued or floated downward at times.

A few very good opportunities are appearing internationally for sophisticated investors who know a good deal about finance, particularly about loans, and who are willing to investigate the risk thoroughly and take every precaution to avoid loss.

As a recent example, an Austrian manufacturer of top-quality electric light bulbs needed a large amount of working capital. Its credit was good, but bank credit was insufficient to take care of its needs. A group of private lenders in New York agreed to lend $160,000 in a series of notes, each one for $10,000 coming due each month. The rate was close to 2 percent per month for the interest on the loan. The finance group sent an investigator to Vienna to verify the existence of the light bulbs that were being financed, and a thorough audit of the inventory was made. In addition, the bulbs were placed in a warehouse and were to be released only against payment—$10,000 worth of bulbs would be released after each $10,000 note was paid. Finally, title to the bulbs was transferred to the lenders so that the manufacturer could not sell the bulbs while failing to pay off the notes. The collateral, which was the bulbs, represented a loan in the amount of 8 cents per bulb. Each bulb retailed for about 65 cents.

A great deal of work was involved in this loan, but there were many silent partners who did not actually investigate the risk, take precautions, and collect the payments. These functions were the responsibility of the managing partner, the finance company head who syndicated the loan. Unless one has a trusted and efficient managing partner, such investments are hardly for the usual investor.

There are several opportunities in the present investment market to secure returns of 12 percent per annum and more, and it is necessary to secure high returns if the overall plan to build wealth is to be worked out in the form of a balanced investment program.

CHAPTER 9

Using Trusts to Preserve Wealth

Amassing wealth is one thing. Holding on to it is quite another matter. One of the preferred methods of preserving wealth is to establish a trust. In this way estate, inheritance, and income taxes can be minimized.

In addition to reducing taxes, trusts can accomplish other objectives for the individual, the family, and others for whom one wishes to assure an income or an accumulation of capital. These objectives most often are:

- Making orderly, thought-out provision for others, usually in the future.
- Facilitating the passing of one's estate to others.
- Serving a public purpose in the assistance of charities, although the most recent tax law has changed the trust function in this connection rather significantly.

For these reasons the use of trusts is widespread, and many banks have entire, often large, departments specializing in them. The New York State Bankers Association even has an independent "trade association" that specializes in the trust functions of its member banks.

Still, the number of trusts is probably miniscule compared with their potential use. If they were properly informed about trusts, it is likely that many more people would profitably use them, and this use could extend downward quite far to potential users at relatively low levels of wealth and income.

There are two main reasons for the limited use of trusts at present. The first is that trust law is somewhat difficult for the layman to understand; and it is also sometimes difficult even for the trust specialist to understand.

The second reason is that the establishment of a trust entails the giving up of one's wealth, or giving up all control or at least some control of it. Almost everyone parts with wealth or its control reluctantly, even though it can be demonstrated that such a course would benefit the individual or the family, or both.

The estate-planning trust

The most common use of the trust is as a tool for carrying out an individual's wishes expressed in a will. This kind of trust is called a testamentary trust and it is administered by a trustee, who may be an individual, a bank, a trust company, or any combination of these. If the trust is set up during the lifetime of the individual, it is called an *inter vivos* (among the living) trust.

A usual objective of the testamentary trust is to provide an income for the decedent's spouse or children. The spouse's income may continue until death, when the corpus (the trust assets) can be turned over to the children; or the income from the trust can go to the children until a particular time when the corpus of the trust can be turned over to them. This latter can occur when they reach their majority or at any other designated time.

On the other hand, the trust can simply be a vehicle for building up capital through nonpayment of income taxes or through only a partial payment of such taxes.

The big objective of the testamentary trust has been to minimize the estate tax. This federal tax begins with an 18 percent rate on estates of under $10,000, for a tax of $1,800. An estate of $100,000 is taxed $23,800. An estate of $1 million is taxed $345,800. A $5 million estate is taxed at $2,550,000, and above $5 million, the tax is 70 percent.

The estate tax is, however, not as severe as it appears. When one arrives at the bottom line and must pay the tax due, there is a credit that can be used in part instead of an all-cash payment to the Internal Revenue Service. For 1977 this "unified credit" is $30,000. In effect, this credit protects $120,667 worth of an estate, so that $120,667 can go to the heirs tax-free.

In 1978 the credit amounts to $34,000, which, in effect, protects $134,000 of an estate. In 1979 the credit rises to $38,000, which shields $147,333 in inheritance. By 1980 the credit rises to $42,500 and shields $161,563. Finally, in 1981 and thereafter, the credit becomes $47,000, which protects $175,625 of the estate passing to the heirs.

In another respect the estate tax is not as harsh as it might appear. There is the so-called marital deduction, which the latest tax reform act has liberalized. Funds can be left to one's spouse without having to be diminished by the estate tax. The amount that can be passed to a spouse in this way is $250,000 or one-half of the adjusted gross estate, whichever is greater.

Thus, if a man leaves an estate of $250,000 to his widow, she pays no estate tax. If he leaves $300,000 to her, then $250,000 is free of estate tax. If he leaves an estate of $1 million, then one-half of the estate—$500,000—can go to his widow free of the estate tax, and various credits can be applied to the other $500,000 left to the widow to minimize the estate tax impact. When the widow is the inheritor, a trust can be employed to minimize the estate tax on the amount of the inheritance that is not protected in these ways.

As regards the entire estate left to the widow, a difficulty arises when she dies, as there is no marital deduction available at that time to protect what she leaves to her children or to anyone else. Of course, the widow may have remarried, in which case the marital deduction can apply again.

At the time the husband dies, the estate tax must be paid, whether or not his estate or any part of it goes into a testamentary trust created at his death.

The generation-skipping trust

While it is possible to extend the operation of the trust beyond the generation of the decedent's sons and daughters, to be free of the estate tax the trust can go to only one generation younger than the person who set it up. So-called generation-skipping trusts can be set up to operate from sons and daughters to grandchildren to great-grandchildren, and so on, ad infinitum, but not without paying the estate tax along the way. Tax-free generation-skipping trusts are not allowed, a generation-skipping trust being defined as one with two or more generations of beneficiaries belonging to generations younger than that of the person who set up the trust.

For example, a trust set up for the benefit of a widow, with the remainder going to a grandchild, is not a generation-skipping trust, because only one younger generation is involved, not two or more. The same trust for the benefit of the widow could be set up with the remainder going to a great-grandchild. Here too only one younger generation is involved, even though the generation is very much younger.

Transfers to grandchildren are given a special tax advantage if they are made through the decedent's son or daughter. It is possible to transfer $250,000 through one's child to one's grandchild. Two such transfers can be made if the decedent has two children. Thus a maximum of $500,000 can be transferred to the grandchildren in this way without the application of the tax. In general the tax applies only to transfers made to succeeding generations after April 30, 1976. Thus, generation-skipping trusts set up before this date are exempt from the tax.

With the exemptions in dollar amounts passed on to one's children and other direct heirs, at some point an estate tax or its equivalent must be paid on funds left in trust to younger generations. This unhappy event takes place at the "end of the line," when there is nobody to leave any money to in succeeding generations. At that point the contents of the trust are added to the rest of the estate of the last heir who dies, and the tax is paid, but the tax on what is in the trust is paid out of the funds of the trust, not out of the rest of the decedent's estate.

Where the trust clearly comes under the new definition of a generation-skipping trust, the generation-skipping tax—about the same as the estate tax—must be paid at the time the generation is "skipped."

In the case in which a trust has been created for the benefit of the grandchild of the grantor, with what is left in the trust going to the great-grandchild on the demise of the grandchild, the tax is paid at the time of the demise of the grandchild. The trust property is included in the grandchild's estate for tax purposes, but the actual payment comes out of the funds in the trust. The amount of the tax is determined, however, by adding the trust property to the rest of the property of the grandchild.

A common plan is to set up a trust for the children with the income going to the widow. When the children reach their majority they can receive some income and at some later time they can receive the entire contents of the trust.

It can be stipulated that if the widow remarries she

shall receive no further income from the trust. At that time, all income can go to the children. It is also possible to stipulate that when the widow remarries she must appoint a trustee only from among the children or other heirs.

It is possible to set up an *inter vivos* trust that can be excluded from the deceased's estate. Such a trust must be irrevocable. The person establishing the trust cannot receive income from it, cannot control it, and cannot receive any other benefits from the trust. This type of transaction is considered to be a taxable gift which may either reduce the "unified credit" available at the death of the grantor, or, if large enough, create a tax liability. Gift tax rules are quite complex, and a specialist should be consulted in advance of any sizable gifts.

It is also possible to set up a revocable *inter vivos* trust. The person establishing such a trust can receive the income, control the trust, and revoke the trust. Such a trust is, however, fully taxable to the estate upon the person's demise.

The life insurance trust

A life insurance trust can contain assets other than the life insurance policy that is its main asset. If there are other assets whose earnings pay the premiums on the policy, it is called a funded life insurance trust. If such paying assets are not in the trust, it is called an unfunded life insurance trust.

In an unfunded trust the insured person pays the premiums as they come due, using "tax-paid dollars." In other words, the person pays income tax on his or her earnings, and out of this tax-paid income, writes checks to the insurance company to cover the premiums.

The life insurance trust is a tax-paying entity, and in most cases would be in a lower tax bracket than that of the head of the family. If the funded life insurance trust has $10,000 worth of bonds in it in addition to the life insurance policy, the bonds may pay, say, $800 a year. After the low income tax on this sum is paid, all or part of the remainder of the $800 goes to pay the premium on the life insurance policy. The "grantor" (the person who establishes the trust) and the payer of the insurance premiums should not be the same individual. Otherwise, it is not possible to take advantage of the low income tax rate of the assets in the trust. All dividends earned by the policy must be applied to the premiums and not taken by the grantor whose life is insured by the policy.

The main objective of such a trust is to get the matured life insurance policy out of the grantor's estate for estate tax purposes.

The widow is often the chief beneficiary of the life insurance policy. She may be given the right to borrow on the policy in the trust for the purpose of paying the premiums on the policy. If she borrows, the interest on her loan may be deductible from her annual income when she computes her income tax.

A life insurance trust can be established by the decedent's will, not to avoid the estate tax, but simply to hold and preserve the estate's assets for the heirs. The proceeds of the insurance policy can be invested by the trustee for the benefit of the heirs.

In order to get a life insurance policy out of one's estate for estate tax purposes, the "incidence of ownership" must be assigned to the trust or to someone else with no strings of any kind attached to the assignment. The insured person cannot pay the premiums and at the same time be certain that the policy will not end up taxed in the estate at the time of death.

The irrevocable life insurance trust can be used for another purpose—to purchase assets from the estate of the decedent at the time of death.

A number of years ago the head of a large family died, leaving an enormous home in Bronxville, New York. The value placed on the home by the Internal Revenue Service for estate tax purposes was $200,000. The property taxes were almost $6,000 a year and the heating bill in cold months amounted to about $700 per month.

A long time after the estate tax was paid, the house was sold to this writer—for a net to the estate of $60,000. Included in the sale was a large Sarouk carpet which had cost $8,800 and was probably worth close to that figure at the time. The same estate included a fine Miami Beach house, which eventually brought $55,000—also far under the estate tax value.

An irrevocable life insurance trust can be set up for the purpose of buying such properties with the money received from the life insurance policy at the demise of the owner of the properties. The trust can be both the owner of the life insurance policy and the beneficiary of the policy. The trust can be directed to use the cash received on the demise of the grantor to buy the properties. The estate would thus have cash to pay the estate tax rather than having two overvalued houses that could well absorb the estate's cash to pay the estate tax. There is no estate tax on the amount in the trust.

The charitable trust

For years colleges and universities have been sending brochures to alumni who seem to be likely sources of donations. The main approach used in these brochures has been to point out that (1) a tax saving will result and that (2) the donor will receive income from the donated property.

The use of the trust in such giving is a refinement that has certain benefits but also certain limitations.

If you place money or other property such as stocks, bonds, or income real estate in a charitable trust for your college you can take an immediate deduction for the amount of the contribution, but not for tangible personal property such as a work of art. If the fund is set up with cash, a deduction for this cash, up to an amount equal to

Contributions to Charities
Double in Decade

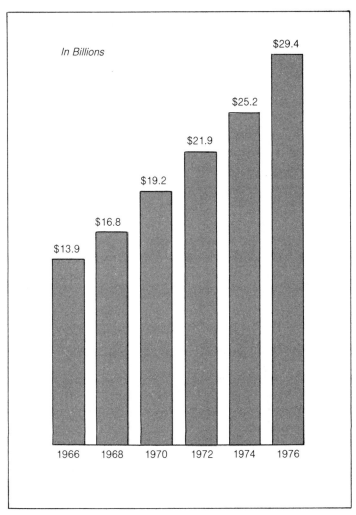

In Billions

1966	$13.9
1968	$16.8
1970	$19.2
1972	$21.9
1974	$25.2
1976	$29.4

Of the total $29.4 billion donated to charity in 1976, individuals contributed $23.6 billion, an increase of 10 percent over 1975. Bequests in wills rose 6 percent to a total of $2.4 billion. The remainder of donations were made by foundations, $2.1 billion, and corporations, over $1.3 billion.

Source: American Association of Fund-Raising Counsel

How the Charitable Pie
Is Apportioned

(Based on contributions in 1976)

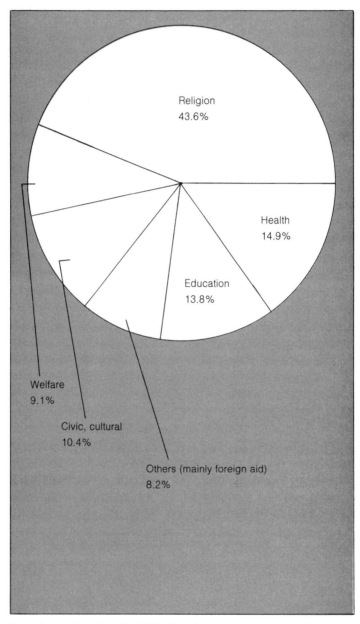

Religion
43.6%

Health
14.9%

Education
13.8%

Welfare
9.1%

Civic, cultural
10.4%

Others (mainly foreign aid)
8.2%

Source: American Association of Fund-Raising Counsel

50 percent of your adjusted gross income is permitted. If the sum contributed to the trust is more than 50 percent of adjusted gross income, then the excess over 50 percent can be carried forward and applied for five successive years. The limit is 30 percent of adjusted gross income for appreciated property, such as stock that has increased in value over the years, with any amount over 30 percent of adjusted gross income of the donor in the year the donation is made carried forward for not more than five years.

The 30 percent deduction from adjusted gross income is not very difficult to get approved by the Internal Revenue Service. The 50 percent deduction is more difficult. A charity to which up to 50 percent of adjusted gross income is donated will be scrutinized by the IRS to learn if enough research is carried on with its funds and if too much of its income is used to pay salaries. If the charity fails one of these tests, the 50 percent limitation may be turned into a 20 percent limitation by the IRS.

One drawback to placing assets in a charitable trust instead of donating it outright is that "present value" must be determined. If the donor is a thirty-year-old man and the charity or the college is to receive the contents of the trust at the time of his death, mortality tables will indicate that the funds will not be received for perhaps forty years. The amount of the contribution must be reduced for tax-deduction purposes by reference to the IRS-approved "present value" tables based on mortality statistics.

The amount of the "discount" of assets placed in a charitable trust depends on the donor's age, on the value of the assets in the trust, and on how much income from the trust the donor plans to receive during the remainder of his or her life. The older the donor is the less the contribution to the trust is "discounted."

At the time the donor dies, the trust is, in effect, not included in the estate. Actually it is included but then a charitable contribution of the amount included in the estate is deducted from the taxable estate. The effect is the elimination of the trust from the estate of the decedent.

One of the big advantages in contributing to one's college in this way is that the income from the trust can go to the donor until death. However, the income is taxed to the donor as it is earned by the property in the trust and distributed to the donor.

There are various refinements of the charitable trust, depending on the objectives of the donor.

A donor who wants a fixed periodic income for life can set up a charitable remainder annuity trust. The income received by the donor will be the same each year even though the trustee may have to invade principal in some years in order to pay the fixed annual amount.

Another variation is the charitable remainder unitrust. Such a trust returns to the person who set it up a fixed percentage of the assets in the trust each year. If the return is to be 5 percent and the assets are $100,000 in a given year, the donor gets $5,000. If the assets rise to $120,000, then the donor gets $6,000 that year.

Still another variation is the net income unitrust. Such a trust pays the donor either the trust's income for the year or a percentage of the fair market value of the assets in the trust, whichever is lower. This type of trust tends to preserve assets. They are not invaded to keep up the income of the donor. At the same time, since the assets are not invaded, the charitable deduction is larger for the person setting up such a trust.

Establishing a short-term trust

In order to qualify for certain tax benefits a short-term trust must be established for a period of at least ten years and one day.

Such a trust can be used as an accumulation trust in this way:

The head of the family can transfer stocks, bonds, or other property that produces income to a trust set up to last at least ten years plus one day. He can name his son as beneficiary of the income. A trustee accumulates the earnings of the trust until the son is twenty-one years of age (provided, of course, that the twenty-first birthday occurs later than ten years and one day after the trust was established). Then the trust ceases to exist. The property that the head of the family put into the trust reverts to him, but the accumulated earnings from the ten years of investment go to the son.

Income earned by the stocks, bonds, or other property in the trust is taxed to the trust, not to the head of the family. Thus the tax bracket is lower and the tax will be lower than if the head of the family added the trust's income to his other income. A gift tax may, however, have to be paid by the head of the family when he sets up the trust.

Since the trust has paid the income tax as income was earned, when the son at age twenty-one receives the accumulated earnings of the trust he pays no income tax on that distribution. If, however, the trust continues past the son's twenty-first birthday, he will have to pay tax on the income earned by the trust after he became twenty-one. Similarly there is a tax to pay if the beneficiary of the trust is someone other than a child. In such a situation a trust is of limited benefit. The person receiving the accumulated and presumably tax-paid earnings of the trust must add the income of the trust to his income and "back-cast" these earnings over the life of the trust, subtracting from his tax liability the tax the trust paid on the income it received while in operation. There seems little or no tax advantage to such a trust.

A maximum of two such short-term trusts can be set up to gain the advantage of a trust's low income tax rates.

Another type of short-term trust can be set up on which the tax is differently applied—but there is still a tax advantage. Such a short-term payout trust can be set up for the benefit of one's parents for the remainder of their lives. Income-producing property such as stocks or bonds is transferred to this trust, and the income earned by the trust is added to the income of the beneficiaries, the parents, not to that of the head of the family. If the income of the parents is low, then the tax will be lower than had the income remained with the head of the family.

When the parents die, the trust property is returned to the head of the family, who had parted with it and its income for only a certain period of time.

Some people are fortunate enough to be lifetime beneficiaries of a trust, perhaps one set up by their parents. Such a beneficiary may well be in a high tax bracket without adding the income of the trust to an already large income. One solution is to make an irrevocable assignment of the income that the trust produces—for at least ten years and one day. The assignee will receive the income and will have to pay the tax on it; and if the assignee is in a lower tax bracket than the assignor, there is an obvious tax saving.

There are many uses and variations of short-term trusts. Income-producing real estate instead of stocks and bonds can be placed in such a trust. If an office building, for example, is placed in a trust, the head of the family can lease back the building and pay rent to the trust. The trust income from his rental of the property is not taxed to him. Instead he gets an income tax deduction for the money he pays to the trust for his rental of the business property.

Spreading income among members of a family results in lower total taxes than when the entire income of a family head is imputed to him and the tax on the income is paid by him. One method of spreading income is the use of multiple payout trusts—not accumulation trusts, but trusts that pay out income as earned.

One might set up such a trust for each of three children and place income-producing assets in each trust. As each trust earns, the income is paid to each child, who presumably is in a lower income tax bracket than the parent. Thus, the total tax saving for a high-income earner who establishes such multiple trusts can be great.

Before establishing any trust with a view to reducing taxes, the best legal opinion obtainable should be sought so that the trust can be set up very carefully. Otherwise, one may find out years after the establishment of the trust that the objective is not acceptable to the Internal Revenue Service.

10

Planning Your Income and Taxes

Annual planning of income and taxes is advisable for almost everyone, certainly the wealth-builder and the would-be wealth-builder, for these reasons:

1. A forecast of your income and taxes for the year ahead will enable you to determine how much you will have available to cover living expenses and provide for savings. A serious error, often made, is spending so much of one's income that, after taxes are paid around April 15, little or nothing remains to meet the goal of adding to capital.

2. If the forecast indicates that income after taxes will be too small to cover living expenses and provide savings, you may want to give some thought to finding a new job or additional sources of income.

3. A forecast of too small an income may make it advisable to shift income from a high-income year to a low year immediately ahead.

4. If the forecast for the year ahead indicates too high an income in relation to the year or years past or the years ahead, possibly because of increased dividends on stock or sale of a piece of real estate at a profit, then you may take steps to shift income from the year ahead to later years.

5. When income for the year ahead seems likely to be high, then a good deal of tax planning may be necessary. Some of the tax shields, which will be discussed later, could be donations to charitable institutions, depreciation of property, business expenses, state and local taxes, real estate taxes, and the foreign tax credit.

Combined planning

While various forms can be used as tools for planning income and taxes, one form combines both kinds of planning. This is the Internal Revenue Service's standard Form 1040, filed by all individuals who pay income tax.

Although tax consultants, attorneys, and accountants certainly have their place in assisting individuals to make out their annual income tax returns, each taxpayer should be completely familiar with his or her own tax return. It is the individual who earns the money, incurs the expenses, and pays the taxes. It is therefore entirely likely that the taxpayer has definite ideas on (1) how income might be planned better for the next year, and (2) what might be done in order to save on the federal income tax. It is obvious from reading Form 1040 what some of the income tax "savers" either are, or might be, with more careful planning.

The preparation of your tax return for the year that has just passed can be excellent practice for the preparation of the same form for the year that lies ahead. In planning for the year ahead, put down on a spare copy of Form

1040 expected income from each source and then determine what the tax on that income will be. The income and expenses can, of course, be only approximations, but approximations using Form 1040 are likely to be vastly more accurate as a guide in determining income and taxes for the year ahead than a rough guess, and even more accurate than careful estimates made without using the form as a guide and base.

The dollars-and-cents planning may of course be done in other ways than by filling in Form 1040 and its subsidiary schedules, but the form is easily available and it is directed to the federal income tax, which is a major element in income planning. Form 1040 is therefore a highly analytical tool from the point of view of income and expense planning.

It is certainly not an indication of competence when an investor finds out, in preparing his tax return for the year just ended, that his income was 64 percent less than the year before. This was the experience of one investor. He paid far less tax than he did in the previous year, but he would have done far better taxwise had he adjusted his income and his expenses so that his income would have been more level year by year. By using Form 1040 as a planning tool, this investor found that for the coming year his income might well be six times what it was in the year just closed—again evidence of poor planning of income, expenses, and taxes.

At first glance Form 1040 looks difficult to prepare and you may feel that the only lines you are able to fill in with confidence are those calling for your name and address. The more you work with the form, however, the clearer it becomes. You develop a kind of expertise, so that each time you prepare the form as a tax return or as a forecast of income, expenses, and taxes, it becomes an easier task. Working with the form involves various "experiments" in order, within possible limits, to adjust income and expenses to minimize taxes. It is worth remembering that it is not at all unusual for an Internal Revenue Service (IRS) agent to audit an income tax return and come to the conclusion that the individual paid too much tax and should be given a refund.

Your preparation of the "pro forma" Form 1040 might result in your finding that too much income or too few expenses appear to fall into the year ahead, and there is too great a tax liability. It may be possible to adjust income or expenses, or both, to reduce the tax, perhaps by increasing income and/or expenses in another year.

Leveling income for each year

An approximately level income, year by year, is one possible result of planning by using Form 1040, even though there may be changes in the IRS regulations for the next taxable year, changes in the instructions to taxpayers, and changes in the law itself.

The first task is to see what your income looks like for the year ahead based on your projection of income and expenses on Form 1040. Little can be done about certain items of income. If you work for wages or a salary, you cannot normally look at the results of your income planning and, if your income appears to be too small, ask for a raise.

Neither can you ask to have your wages or salary postponed if it appears that for this particular year your income will be so large as to place you in an unusually high tax bracket. In any event, the maximum tax on earned income is 50 percent, and shifting small amounts of earnings between years is not really effective in reducing taxes.

Fees can, however, be adjusted. If it appears that current income will place the individual in a high tax bracket, the income recipient may choose not to perform additional services which bring in fees for the rest of the year. Work for new clients may possibly be postponed until the start of the new tax year.

In a reverse way, an effort can be made to perform services for more income before the current tax year ends.

To indicate the benefits of leveling income year by year, let us assume that the income of one individual was $100,000 in 1975. In 1976 the income was $35,000—a drop of 65 percent. If we use current tax rates, we find that the tax on an income of $100,000 for married taxpayers filing a joint return is $45,100. On an income of $35,000, the tax might be about $10,340—$55,440 for the two years. If the $135,000 income for the two years had been equally divided between those years—$67,500 for each year—the tax would have been $25,920 per year, or $51,840 for the two years, a saving of $3,600 in taxes.

In the case of many types of notes receivable, foreign notes included, it is often possible to equalize income. Where income for the current year is low, and income for the next year appears as though it might be high, it may be possible to sell the note before the end of the current year, thus moving the interest income out of the next year.

If income for the next year appears as though it will be high, then maturities can be arranged for the year following, so that maturities for the immediate year ahead are skipped.

In the same way one can sell a part of a mortgage or an entire mortgage and receive income from the sale. One can also sell a fractional interest in a building where depreciation has made possible a sale at a profit from the depreciated base.

Another way to shift income between years is to make capital gains in the year in which they are needed, that is, when they will not raise income to a level so high as to create an undesirable tax liability. Many people own appreciated securities—stocks that have risen recently, or stocks that rose many years ago and fell in the recent recession but have gone up a bit in the present market. It is possible to sell appreciated securities in years of low income in order to equalize income and consequently the income tax.

One advantage in acquiring collectibles is that these too, if they appreciate in value (as almost all have over the past several years), can be sold in order to produce a capital gain for low-income years.

Conversely, capital losses can be taken in years in which there is a capital gain that would tend to make the year a big one for income and taxes. Almost every stock market investor has some stocks that have gone down instead of up. No one invariably picks winners in the stock market.

The capital gain is the ideal way to equalize income because only half is taxed, the one-half of the capital gain being added to all other income for tax calculation.

The alternate way to figure capital gains is to apply a tax of 25 percent to all capital gains of up to $50,000 a year. Capital gains in excess of $50,000 are taxed at a rate of 35 percent. The maximum capital gains tax is, however, often above this 35 percent rate. If "preference items" in your income exceed $10,000 in the tax year or one-half of the amount of income taxes you pay, whichever figure is greater, you must pay a minimum tax of 15 percent.

The so-called preference items include one-half of long-term capital gains, accelerated depreciation on all leased personal property, and itemized deductions that total more than 60 percent of your adjusted gross income on page one of Form 1040 (with the exception of medical and casualty deductions). There are also preference items associated with petroleum production and other specialized types of investments.

The result of the lower exclusion for preference items and the raising of the minimum tax to 15 percent is that capital gains can now be taxed at a rate of up to 43 percent.

Thus, if you want to take a big capital gain you might well save it for a year of low income or a year in which you can offset the capital gain with a capital loss.

The total capital gains tax liability should be figured on Form 1040 in planning income, expenses, and taxes.

The two elements of capital gains and ordinary income are totaled and brought forward to page one of Form 1040. Income other than wages, dividends, and interest are added together. A few adjustments can be made for moving expenses, an employee's business expenses (which are very limited for income tax purposes), and payment into a Self-Employed Individuals Tax Retirement Act plan.

When all of the adjustments applicable in the year have been made, you arrive at a basic and highly important figure—the adjusted gross income—and on this figure a number of computations can be made by the planner to minimize the income tax.

Itemizing deductions

Your adjusted gross income is also entered on the first line of Part III on the back of page one of Form 1040. You are now ready to subtract your itemized deductions so that you can arrive at the all-important figure of taxable income, on which the actual tax is based.

One of the most significant areas in which to plan income, expenses, and taxes is contributions. Appreciated property of all kinds can be contributed to charitable institutions, educational institutions, and museums. Generally, a deduction of up to 30 percent of adjusted gross income is allowed for the fair market value of appreciated property, whether it be securities, a painting, or almost anything else that is worth more than it cost. The appraised market value is the basis of the deduction.

Appreciated property may be taxed at rates ranging from 25 percent or even less to 43 percent if sold at a profit which results in a capital gain. One has the alternative of paying a 25 percent tax on a capital gain of $50,000 or less or adding half of the capital gain (no matter how high it is) to ordinary income. Thus, a person who had a low annual income of, say, $8,000 and a capital gain of $10,000 would add half of this capital gain, $5,000, to the $8,000 of ordinary income, making a reportable income of $13,000, to which, after allowable deductions, the ordinary income tax rate would apply.

Another alternative is to donate the appreciated property and deduct the appraised market value from adjusted gross income, thus reducing the federal income tax. This is one area in which planning income and taxes, using Form 1040 as a working document, can be of considerable benefit.

A few years ago the estate of Edith Halpert was sold. Mrs. Halpert was a New York dealer in modern paintings. One painting in the estate had cost $2,000 when she purchased it a number of years before the auction sale of her paintings took place. At the auction this painting sold for $175,000. Had the painting been donated to a museum, that much tax credit would have protected an income of $580,000 ($175,000 is a little more than 30 percent of $580,000, and we assume an adjusted gross income of $580,000). The remainder—$405,000—would have been taxable.

Without the tax protection of the donation the tax might have amounted to $376,000 (but we do not know the rest of Mrs. Halpert's income for that year, of course).

With the $175,000 deduction the tax might have been $253,000. Thus, the tax saving through donation of this one painting might have been as high as $123,000. If one sold the painting that cost $2,000 for $175,000, paid a capital gains tax of 40 percent, and kept what remained, that remainder would be about $105,000.

Adjusted gross income can be reduced through a donation by 50 percent rather than 30 percent—if the appreciation in the item donated is reduced by 50 percent.

Thus, the donor of a painting valued at $100,000 that cost $2,000 can reduce the appreciation of $98,000 by one-half to $49,000, and this sum will protect an adjusted gross income of double this amount. It will reduce an adjusted gross income of $98,000 to $49,000 for tax purposes.

Other significant deductions from the point of view of substantial tax saving, are real estate taxes and state and local income taxes, including state capital gains taxes. The figures of the year just past might be used for planning these on Form 1040.

Sales taxes and the gasoline tax generally do not amount to much, and last year's figures can probably be used for projecting taxes for the year ahead.

Business expenses

Of all business expenses that may be deducted from income for tax purposes, travel and transportation can amount to the greatest sum. From one point of view it might be desirable to have a business, either part-time or full-time, that requires travel and the use of an automobile. If, for instance, one is an expert on the art and antique market, secures an income from it in the form of fees or as capital gains, and travels to various places in this country and abroad in connection with art and antiques, a major portion of the travel expenses is deductible from income for tax purposes. A daily diary and expense sheets are useful documents to back up deductions for business travel in case of an audit by the Internal Revenue Service.

· With automobile allowances by the IRS now 15 cents a mile for the first 15,000 miles of strictly business travel and 10 cents a mile for every mile over 15,000, automobile expenses for business purposes can provide a substantial tax shield—for either full-time or part-time business activities.

Alternatively, one can depreciate a car used for business purposes and also deduct expenses for repairs, gas, oil, insurance, license, and perhaps some other items. The depreciation is the most important element of deductible expenses, and the IRS describes depreciation as a tax shield in this way:

"You are a doctor and drive 20,000 business miles during the year. You have two cars—A and B. Car B was used exclusively for nonbusiness purposes. Car A was purchased new on January 2 for $4,500. Assuming it has a four-year life and a salvage value of $500, a full year's depreciation on it is $1,000 ($4,500 − $500 ÷ 4). If you used Car A exclusively for business, you will be allowed a $1,000 depreciation deduction on Car A only."

One car can, of course, be used for both business and pleasure, and depreciation and other expenses can be prorated for business and nonbusiness uses.

Business entertainment is allowed, but large sums for entertainment may be questioned, as well as whether the people entertained were actually business-connected.

The office in the home allows an allocation of expenses to it which can be deducted from income as a business expense. Under the provisions of the 1976 tax law, however, expenses of the office at home have been circumscribed considerably.

To be tax-deductible, the office in your home must be your principal place of business or the place where you normally meet with patients, clients, or customers. The office must be used regularly and exclusively for that purpose. It cannot, for instance, be a recreation room in which on occasion you do some work. The self-employed person can certainly meet all of these tests, and all expenses allocated to the office can be deducted, including electricity, heating, repairs to the house, depreciation, and possibly other items.

If you are an employee, your office at home must exist

The Income Tax Bite
Taken by States

	At $10,000 of Annual Income	At $17,500 of Annual Income	At $25,000 of Annual Income
Alabama	$147	$ 339	$ 593
Alaska	$182	$ 369	$ 668
Arizona	$148	$ 314	$ 646
Arkansas	$163	$ 387	$ 771
California	$ 64	$ 293	$ 688
Colorado	$157	$ 382	$ 785
Delaware	$236	$ 652	$1,238
D.C.	$250	$ 579	$1,107
Georgia	$ 83	$ 319	$ 714
Hawaii	$212	$ 611	$1,133
Idaho	$138	$ 474	$ 973
Illinois	$150	$ 338	$ 525
Indiana	$150	$ 300	$ 450
Iowa	$295	$ 528	$ 884
Kansas	$126	$ 297	$ 560
Kentucky	$243	$ 444	$ 750
Louisiana	$ 48	$ 125	$ 227
Maine	$ 60	$ 160	$ 359
Maryland	$255	$ 479	$ 812
Massachusetts	$277	$ 641	$1,013
Michigan	–$ 59*	$ 103	$ 221
Minnesota	$543	$1,016	$1,724
Mississippi	$ 38	$ 218	$ 473
Missouri	$109	$ 268	$ 567
Montana	$279	$ 499	$ 947
Nebraska	$ 35	$ 158	$ 330

	At $10,000 of Annual Income	At $17,500 of Annual Income	At $25,000 of Annual Income
New Mexico	$ 84	$ 238	$ 527
New York	$206	$ 550	$1,174
North Carolina	$258	$ 535	$1,000
North Dakota	$105	$ 338	$ 822
Ohio	$ 55	$ 188	$ 390
Oklahoma	$ 50	$ 196	$ 517
Oregon	$238	$ 633	$1,184
Pennsylvania	$200	$ 350	$ 500
Rhode Island	$119	$ 286	$ 521
South Carolina	$157	$ 420	$ 885
Utah	$148	$ 452	$ 821
Vermont	$216	$ 520	$ 946
Virginia	$175	$ 449	$ 829
West Virginia	$144	$ 276	$ 494
Wisconsin	$365	$ 801	$1,488

These tax figures are for a married couple with two children. It is assumed that all income is from wages and salaries earned by one spouse. At $10,000, the optional standard deduction is used. At $17,500, itemized deductions of $3,520 are used. At $25,000, deductions of $4,365 are assumed. For states that allow a deduction for federal income taxes, these deductions were made: $791 at $10,000, $1,908 at $17,500, and $3,470 at $25,000. Ten states did not levy a general personal income tax in 1974, the latest year for which figures are available. They are Connecticut, Florida, Nevada, New Hampshire, New Jersey, South Dakota, Tennessee, Texas, Washington, and Wyoming. New Jersey now levies an income tax. Figures for Michigan are based only on taxes of Detroit homeowners.

* Refund of other taxes by state.

Source: Advisory Commission on Intergovernmental Relations

for the convenience of your employer. A part-time free lance or a part-time consultant is not likely to be allowed any deductions for an office at home.

On the other hand, in the case of a restorer of paintings and furniture who was also an artist and conducted art classes in his huge home in Virginia, a representative of the Internal Revenue Service inspected the house and decided that two-thirds of all expenses of the home could be allocated to the business and thus deducted from income on Form 1040.

Using depreciation

Although depreciation is certainly a business expense and might well have been included in the previous section of this chapter, it is so important from a tax point of view as to merit separate treatment.

Accelerated depreciation was developed for the purpose of accomplishing certain economic results. What accelerated depreciation amounts to is more depreciation in the early years of the life of a property. The result is a good many dollars of tax shield early in the depreciable life of properties used for business purposes. This shield can be used by investors in commercial properties such as apartment houses and office buildings as well as by homeowners who lease their dwellings.

In the case of a large apartment house in Atlantic City, New Jersey, investments of as little as $28,000 were accepted from individuals. The money was invested gradually over a period of three years, so that a wide group of investors could be tapped for part-ownership. For the first three years the depreciation shield was so large that no investor had to pay much tax on the income from this property, yet the nominal return on the building, before depreciation, was about 12 percent per annum. With the authorization of gambling in Atlantic City the building may well be sold for much more than is invested in it.

There is a new restriction on the use of accelerated

depreciation. Such depreciation is called a "preference item," and preference items are now taxed at a rate of 15 percent when they amount to over $10,000 per year or half of regular taxes paid, whichever is greater. In the future, straight-line depreciation may be used more than it is at present because it does not involve the special preference item tax. Thus, if the owner rents a $200,000 home, of which the land is worth $100,000 and the structure $100,000, it may be possible to depreciate the structure over twenty years at 5 percent or $5,000 per year. The contents may be depreciated over six years. If the contents are worth $30,000, one-sixth—$5,000—may be the depreciation charge each year. The total annual depreciation of $10,000 on the house and the contents can thus provide quite a sizable tax shield.

In addition, property taxes are fully deductible from income before the income tax is computed. These taxes can be deducted even by the homeowner who does not rent out the property.

In the same way, interest on the mortgage can be deducted. The homeowner can deduct this interest even though the house is not rented.

If we combine maintenance expenses, depreciation, interest, and property taxes, we find a total deduction from income that can provide an enormous shield against the income tax. Total expenses can easily cover a large sum received for renting out one's house and still leave a red figure to be deducted from other income, as explained in Chapter 5.

Foreign tax credit

One of the reasons foreign investments, particularly foreign loans and deposits, have been popular is the income tax imposed by the foreign government, paradoxical though this may seem.

As an example we might cite the Mexican income tax. The Mexican government has a basic tax rate of 10 per-

Form 1116

(Rev. Dec. 1976)

Department of the Treasury
Internal Revenue Service

Computation of Foreign Tax Credit

Individual, Fiduciary, or Nonresident Alien Individual

For calendar year 19......., or other taxable year beginning ...., 19......., and ending ...., 19 ....

Attach to Form 1040, 1041, or 1040NR

Name — Social security number

Address (Number and street) — Employer identification number

City or town, State and ZIP code or Country

Resident of (Name of country)

Citizen of (Name of country)

This form is being completed for credit with respect to:

(Use a separate Form 1116 for each type of income. See General Instruction J.)

- [ ] Nonbusiness (section 904(d)) interest income
- [ ] Dividends from a DISC or former DISC
- [ ] Foreign oil and gas extraction income
- [ ] Income from sources within U.S. possessions (limitation method ▶ [ ] per-country OR [ ] overall)
- [ ] All other income from sources outside the U.S.

Schedule A—Taxable Income from Sources Outside the U.S.

1. Name of Foreign Country or U.S. Possession (Use a separate line for each)	2. Gross Income from Sources Outside the U.S.							
	(a) Dividends	(b) Gross Rents and Royalties	(c) Foreign Source Capital Gain Net Income (See Instruction K)	(d) Wages, Salaries and Other Employee Compensation	(e) Business or Profession (Sole Proprietorship)	(f) Gross Income from Trusts and Estates	(g) Other (Including Interest) (Attach schedule)	(h) Total (Add columns (a) through (g))
A								
B								
C								
D								
E								
F								
G								
Totals (add lines A through G)								

3. Applicable Deductions and Losses

	Directly Allocable Deductions						4. Taxable Income or (Loss) from Sources Outside the U.S. (before recapture of prior year overall foreign losses) (Column 2(h) less column 3(g))
	(a) Expenses Directly Allocable to Business or Profession	(b) Depreciation and Depletion Directly Allocable to Rent and Royalty Income	(c) Repairs and Other Expenses Directly Allocable to Rent and Royalty Income	(d) Other Expenses Directly Allocable to Specific Income Items (Attach schedule)	(e) Ratable Share of All Other Deductions Not Directly Allocable (Attach schedule)	(f) Losses from Foreign Sources	(g) Total Applicable Deductions and Losses (Add columns (a) through (f))
A							
B							
C							
D							
E							
F							
G							
Totals							

1. Credit is claimed for taxes			2. Type of Tax	3. Statute Imposing Tax (Title, number, section, etc.) (identify in detail)	4. Foreign Taxes Paid or Accrued (Attach receipt or copy of return) (See General Instruction H.)								5. Reduction for Taxes on Income Excluded under Section 911. Foreign Mineral Income and for Failure to Furnish Returns Required under Section 6038 (Also See General Instruction N)
☐ Paid ☐ Accrued					In Foreign Currency				In U.S. Dollars (See instruction for Schedule B, column 4.)				
Date Paid	Date Accrued				Tax Withheld at Source on:		(c) Other Foreign Taxes Paid or Accrued	(d) Conversion Rate (Attach schedule)	Tax Withheld at Source on:		(g) Other Foreign Taxes Paid or Accrued	(h) Total Foreign Taxes Paid or Accrued (Add cols. (e), (f), and (g))	
					(a) Dividends	(b) Rents and Royalties			(e) Dividends	(f) Rents and Royalties			
A													
B													
C													
D													
E													
F													
G													

Totals (add lines A through G) . . . .

Schedule C—Computation of Foreign Tax Credit

1 Total foreign taxes paid or accrued (from Schedule B, column 4(h), "Totals" line) . . . . .
2 Carryback or carryover (attach schedule showing computation in detail) (see General Instruction L) .
3 Reduction for taxes (from Schedule B, column 5, "Totals" line) . . . .
4 Total foreign taxes available for credit (line 1 plus line 2 less line 3) . . . .
5 Taxable income or (loss) from sources outside the U.S. (from Schedule A, column 4, "Totals" line). (If loss, omit lines 6 through 18) .
6 Recapture of prior year overall foreign losses (see General Instruction K) . . . .
7 Net foreign source taxable income (line 5 less line 6) . . . .
8 Taxable income from all sources (enter taxable income from your tax return—Form 1040, 1040NR or 1041) .
9 Deduction taken on your tax return for personal exemptions . . . .
10 Add line 8 and line 9 . . . .
11 Divide line 7 by line 10 (if line 7 exceeds line 10, enter the figure "1") . . . .
12 Total U.S. income tax before any credits (see General Instruction D) . . . .
13 General tax credit . . . .
14 Credit for the elderly . . . .
15 Add line 13 and line 14 . . . .
16 Line 12 less line 15 . . . .
17 Limitation on credit (line 16 multiplied by line 11) . . . .
18 Foreign tax credit (line 4 or line 17, whichever is less) . . . .

Schedule D—Summary of Credits from Separate Schedules C

1 Credit with respect to nonbusiness (section 904(d)) interest . . . .
2 Credit with respect to dividends from a DISC or former DISC . . . .
3 Credit with respect to foreign oil and gas extraction income. . . . .
4 Credit with respect to income from sources within U.S. possessions . . . .
5 Credit with respect to all other income from sources outside the U.S. . . . .
6 Total (add lines 1 through 5) . . . .
7 Reduction in credit for international boycott operations (see General Instruction N) . . . . . .
8 Foreign tax credit (line 6 less line 7). Enter here and on your tax return . . . .

cent for interest on deposits and loans, including deposits and loans made in Mexico by foreigners. In some cases the tax is 21 percent. To the basic tax is added another tax of 5.75 percent. These taxes are not based on income. They are flat percentages charged to small income earners and to multimillionaires alike. The investor can, however, use the tax credit to pay U.S. income tax, with certain limitations as to how much of it can be used in any year, a limitation that is not very serious.

Since international interest rates have been 12 percent, 15 percent, and even as high as 18 percent net, the lender has received 12 percent or more plus the tax credit.

The tax, in effect, can amount to two percentage points, and even more in the case of Brazil and certain other countries. The two percentage points are an addition to the nominal interest rate of 12 percent or 15 percent or whatever the net rate is. Investors therefore have often been willing to take a big chance on currency drops in foreign countries in order to receive the high yield plus the tax credit.

In the case of foreign income and the foreign income tax credit the working tool is Internal Revenue Service Form 1116, a fairly complicated form, until one learns how to fill it in through a few years of using it. The foreign tax credit can provide enormous assistance in paying the U.S. income tax and in shielding income against taxes.

Some foreign investment and deposit opportunities have been described in Chapter 8, and such opportunities are still available to even the smaller investor.

Income and tax planning summarized

Income and tax planning, in summary, can aid significantly in these ways:

- Indicate that income might be reduced by shifting it to lower income years than the one for which the planning is being done.

• Indicate that efforts should be made to increase income for the year ahead if it is too low in relation to income for other years.

• Indicate that because income appears likely to be high in the year being planned for, all possible tax shields should be employed. Some of these shields are: donations to charitable institutions, educational institutions, and museums; depreciation of property; business expenses for travel, automobile, and office; real estate taxes and other state and local taxes; and the foreign tax credit.

Possible tax shields are numerous and complicated, but all of those suggested above are relatively simple. The Internal Revenue Service has audited a large number of returns employing these shields and has accepted them in the course of many years. When used properly, such tax shields can greatly assist in building capital.

11

25 Rules for Building Wealth

It is not as difficult to become wealthy as is generally believed. The fact is that many people of average education and intelligence have succeeded in amassing fortunes.

If it were not for a number of negative personal reasons, many more people would have accumulated wealth. We might list these reasons in summary form:

1. *They cannot visualize themselves as being wealthy.* If you cannot establish this positive attitude of attaining wealth, it is hard to get started in wealth-building. Lacking this visualization, most people do not even attempt a wealth-building program.

2. *They believe the much-quoted fallacy, "You have to have money to make money."* This is the most common

reason given by people to explain why they do not have money. As a matter of fact, a number of the students of this writer, when he was a professor of investments, said their parents had explained to them that one needed a good amount of money to start with in order to make money. So ingrained was this idea in these students that it could not be eliminated, even when they were given examples of how wealth had been built fairly rapidly from virtually nothing. Some money is helpful at the start, of course, but it is not indispensable, and one does not need a million dollars to make a million dollars.

When the mobile home finance and insurance plan was developed by this writer a number of years ago, he and his wife opened a bank account with just a few hundred dollars. The banks then sent in checks—some very large ones—for insurance premiums. This special premium account built very rapidly into five and six figures, and the commissions received from these premiums were then placed in an account which quickly reached five figures. A wealth-building program was well under way.

If it were necessary to have money in order to make money, many, if not most, of the wealthy people in the United States would still be poor!

3. *They find it too hard to break out of their present routine.* As a person stays in a job and grows older, it becomes harder and harder to change the nine-to-five routine. It becomes fixed in the mind of the employee that the time to do business is nine-to-five, and only nine-to-five. During these hours all work must be done exclusively for the employer since the employee's time is bought for this period.

Every evening is spent in relaxation, and this relaxation is thought to be necessary in order to prepare for work the next day. The evening is not viewed as an opportunity to work for oneself in any way. Otherwise one might become "overtired."

Weekends are even more a time for relaxation. They

must provide a complete change so that the employee can arrive at work Monday at 9:00 A.M. fit for a full week's work from nine-to-five until the following Friday at 5:00 P.M.

4. *They cannot discipline themselves enough to start accumulating wealth.* To work when one arrives home around 6:00 P.M. and to get up on Saturday morning and work at anything, even wealth planning, requires an amount of self-discipline that few people have. Work habits, including some evening and weekend work, are best developed during one's school years, especially during the college years; but in recent times a great deal of emphasis at many colleges was in the other direction—away from the "Puritan work ethic." Students were propagandized into believing that work was, at least, unpleasant and that to "really live" they should work moderately, which often meant "work as little as you can get by with."

Without a good deal of self-discipline you cannot build wealth—or build anything else, for that matter.

5. *They are lazy.* Laziness is a key element in the failure to build wealth, and it is somewhat different from the above-mentioned failure to discipline oneself.

Laziness is a word which is not much used today. Any work is to a degree demanding, and it is far easier to sit around doing nothing or to indulge in pleasure than to work; but without forcing oneself to give something one cannot get something in return.

Laziness may be so much a part of one's makeup that nothing can be done about it. On the other hand, the effects of laziness may be minimized, and one may set a schedule to work on wealth-building activities, including setting the alarm clock to prevent sleeping until noon on Saturday and Sunday.

6. *They lack intellectual curiosity.* Most people do only what they know how to do and what they have been doing in the past. They won't bother to look for new opportunities.

One New York real estate man who had accumulated a multimillion-dollar fortune stated in early 1970: "There are three important investment areas: the stock market, petroleum, and real estate. I don't know anything about the stock market or about petroleum. I do know about real estate and this is the area in which I operate."

He operated well and profitably until the great real estate debacle of 1973-75. He did not get out of real estate. He did not diversify. He did not look for anything else. And he, like so many other real estate investors, got into serious trouble when the real estate market and the mortgage market declined.

7. *They have the feeling that they are just average.* They feel that wealth-building is beyond their capabilities since they believe that such activity is for the superintelligent or the ultradynamic, not for the average person.

8. *They are "income oriented" and not "wealth oriented."* Most Americans believe that the measure of business success is how much one makes (salary or fees) per year. The $80,000-a-year executive is thus twice as successful as the $40,000-a-year executive, by this generally accepted measure.

Wealth-building, however, is often done by placing funds in things that increase in value "very quietly." It may not even be expedient to sell the things and thus add to the income or capital gains of a particular year. Remember the man mentioned in Chapter 1 who probably never had a salaried income above $12,000 a year When his job was eliminated in 1975 he ceased working, at age fifty, and may never work again. He does not need to work. His collection of paintings and drawings has very quietly increased in value over a period of years. By selling one or two of his paintings or drawings each year he will be able to live luxuriously for the rest of his life, never showing much income or much capital gain for any particular year.

9. *Their diversions defeat their aspirations to wealth.*

One of the main diversions is liquor. Drugs are also a deterrent to breaking out of any routine and moving up the wealth ladder. A few drinks or a few pills and one can be quite content to do nothing—until the effects wear off and time has moved on, leaving the drinker or the drug taker even more certainly relegated to the sidelines of life.

10. *They really do not want to become different from what they are now.* They want to continue doing exactly what they have been doing, and the longer they have been doing it, the more they want to continue doing it. Any other course of action requires too much thought, too much planning, too much time, too much effort for them.

The reverse of this is that people tend to become what they want to become, if they want to become something else strongly enough and for a long enough period of time. If they are not content to sit back in one of life's byways but are always planning for something else, they may well become something else.

Rules for accumulating wealth

Those who do feel strongly committed to the idea of becoming wealthy may find it useful to keep in mind the following summary of rules:

1. *Save.* Saving is basic to virtually all wealth-building. Most new businesses are started with personal savings. In the businesses organized and operated by this writer, he had to save enough to pay his rent and buy his groceries until the new business took hold and produced surplus income. Too many businesses fail because not enough capital is in the business to carry it over the initial loss period. Initial capital acquired from saving need not be great. Whether one puts savings into a new business or into other wealth-building activities makes no difference; it is important to save while building up capital.

2. *Control your expenses.* Expenses tend to creep up with increases in income, almost without regard to how high income is. The result is that wealth is never accumulated. Expense books are a first and easy step to controlling cash outgo, as each month you can see only too clearly what the expenditures have been. From here, you can proceed to an elaborate system of budgeting, although an elaborate system is by no means necessary.

3. *Watch your family outlays very carefully.* It is easy to decide in conjunction with your family that it would be nice to have a larger or more modern house or one in a better community, or to buy a new and finer car or a boat, or whatever is desired. Every family is constantly faced with the necessity to make decisions involving a large immediate cash outlay or an outlay on the time-payment plan with periodic payments that eat into the ability to save and invest.

An answer is to declare a moratorium on any capital outlays or any new obligations for capital assets for a period of time. At the end of, say, a year, the situation can be reviewed and purchases made if thought necessary. When these purchases are finally made it is a good idea to choose with the idea of investment value whenever possible. A house, for example, and its furnishings, as well as a car, jewelry, and other articles can be chosen from an investment standpoint. In this way the choice may be affected, and the entire family can become aware of what constitutes a good investment.

4. *Stick with your wealth-building program all the time.* Wealth-building is not a minor activity to be thought about casually when one has nothing better to do. Concentrate on the goals of saving, investing wisely, and building capital. At one point this writer kept a personal financial statement (balance sheet) and brought it up to date every day. Noting one's net worth daily can encourage saving and wealth-building.

5. *Get up early and start working on your wealth-*

building activities. When reading biographies or news articles about successful people, one often learns that they rise at 5:00 or 6:00 in the morning, take a brisk walk or do exercises or swim, and arrive at their offices at, say, 7:30 or 8:00. This should also be the schedule for wealth-builders who work at home before going to their regular employment. The best work is often done in the morning with a fresh mind and a good deal of energy. An hour a day on the activity of building one's fortune amounts to five or six hours a week and perhaps 250 hours a year—for which time one may expect some positive results.

6. *Discuss the wealth-building program with your family.* Without the wholehearted cooperation of your spouse, you may not get far with your program. Some married people keep separate bank accounts on the theory that what their mate does not know will not hurt their wealth-building activities; but a thoroughgoing program of wealth-building usually requires family cooperation. The entire undertaking then becomes a team effort and you are not working without help.

7. *Study, read, analyze, and discuss wealth-building with wealth-builders and with those who can help you build wealth.* The more "homework" you do, the better is likely to be the result in terms of wealth-building. You must devote time and energy to investigation of wealth-building activities if you are to succeed in wealth accumulation. Wealth accumulation is a business like any other business. You must work at it constantly. Associate with those who can be of assistance, and study reports, newsletters, magazines, newspapers, and books dealing with the field of your activities. Don't overlook your local library.

8. *Use your fear of failure.* Fear is, of course, an unpleasant emotion, but the person who fears failure usually makes extra efforts to succeed. Tension is also an unpleasant feeling, and fear creates tension, but as Paul Getty told this writer, "One must learn to live with tension."

Tension is not hard to get used to, and the great tension that Paul Getty felt at times did not seem to weaken his heart or cut his life short. He was running his company as chief executive up to the time of his death in 1976, when he was in his eighties. Paul Getty was not always America's richest man, and there were times when he had difficulty raising even modest sums of money to go into very promising business ventures.

9. *Find a need and fill it.* This advice merits the strongest emphasis. Don't bother with products or services that no one wants or only a few people want. Find an important need of a large number of people and try to satisfy that need.

Among those who have not accumulated wealth the general opinion seems to be that wealth is acquired by stepping on the necks of others. As a matter of fact, most wealth is not won at the expense of others, but through benefit to others.

10. *Be alert to new opportunities.* Do not be like the real estate expert mentioned earlier who knew real estate and not the stock market or petroleum, and insisted on having all his eggs in the real estate basket through the real estate depression of 1973-75. Had he looked over the immense area of business he might have at least diversified if not moved out of real estate altogether.

The same old thing is the easiest thing to do, but times change and what is profitable today may well turn into a loss proposition tomorrow. The more information that comes to your attention the better for your wealth-building activities. This information should cover a diverse group of opportunities—the stock market, the bond market, options, new types of businesses, commodities, art, antiques, real estate, classic cars, to name just some. The more one learns about the various opportunities, the more flexible one becomes and the easier it is to diversify or to move out of one area and into another.

11. *Watch for upward trend signals.* A few years ago a

Duesenberg car made news when it was auctioned for the unprecedented sum of $152,000. This was a signal that an upward trend had begun in the entire field of antique and classic cars. Since that time almost every antique and classic automobile has moved upward in price—by perhaps an average of 50 percent. The Rembrandt that sold for $2.3 million to the Metropolitan Museum of Art in the early 1960s signaled a new era in art as an investment, and in the decade of the 1960s the art market overall tripled in price level.

12. *Sell on a rising market.* Some of the biggest losses have been experienced by people who did not sell on a rising market because they were not content to make a good profit but instead wanted to wring the last dollar of gain from the market. When the market turned down they waited for it to turn up again so they could maximize their profit. They often waited until not only the profit disappeared but much of their capital disappeared too.

One man invested $75,000 in a grocery conglomerate. He watched the value of his stock rise to $1.75 million. He didn't sell. He then watched the stock drop and drop until its value had fallen to $250,000. This still represented a good profit, but hardly comparable to what it would have been had he sold at $1.75 million or anywhere near that figure.

13. *Take a big profit if you can get it regardless of whether the market is rising, falling, or standing still.* One group of financiers, with many centuries of financing experience to draw upon, follows the rule: "Never walk away from a profit." It never hurts to take a profit, but it does hurt to take a loss. It is always stimulating to fancy how fine a profit twice as large might be, but there is always the chance that the investment will go down instead of up. At certain times this principle of taking a profit puts one out of a particular investment or out of a business. Still, capital is not the easiest thing to come by,

and taking even a moderate profit builds one's wealth.

14. *Go on to new things.* If the art market has risen, a wise course of action might be to take a profit on the art you have collected and then go into some new and rising area. The same for antique and classic cars. If you can get $250,000 for your Bugatti Royale and $175,000 for your Duesenberg "J," perhaps the time has come to look for other areas of investment. In many ways the impressionist painting market has not only peaked but gone over the peak, and it might pay to get out of this area and into some other investment, either in the field of art or in another field, even though impressionists may rise again some time in the future.

15. *Don't punish yourself because of your losses.* If you are not willing to take losses, there is a good likelihood that you will not experience large gains. To realize a profit, one must take a risk, and sometimes to realize a big profit one must take a big risk. The investor who cannot accept losses is too conservative to take the chances necessary to make large profits. It would be better for such a person to spend money as it is earned, before its value is diminished by inflation. Reliving one's losses damages a person's willingness to take the chances necessary to make profits. Forget your losses as fast as you can.

16. *Cut your losses as rapidly as you can.* Do not hesitate to pull in your horns if it is the expedient thing to do—if you feel you personally are going to experience hard times or if the country is going through a period of hard times.

If you have made a mistake, admit it to yourself. And don't be afraid to admit your mistakes to your friends. Successful people are often inclined to tell stories of their financial failures. Paul Getty told many such stories. George Delacorte tells them. So does Arthur Murray. It may be a wish to apologize for making so much money that spurs them to tell such stories. Or perhaps it simply represents the pure objectivity of the successful business person. In any event, it is the better part of valor to assess the future dispassionately, decide if you should take your loss and get out, then act, and forget about it so that all of your energies can be devoted to going on to something that looks more promising.

17. *Don't take foolish chances.* A sound principle is to risk a little to make a lot. If you have accumulated $1 million during years of careful business operation and capital-building, don't risk a major part of that $1 million on something new and untried or on something that has a real possibility of resulting in a major loss.

The more capital you have the more cautious you should be with the major part of your capital. You have more, and you thus do not have to accumulate as much as you did when you had less.

18. *Get in and out of certain business situations fast.* If there is a good profit, it may be best to take that profit and get out. If the venture or investment does not work out during a reasonable period of time, get out. Don't try to preserve your image of 100 percent success in every venture. Instead of an image of success, you might well develop an image of failure.

19. *Think of your capital as a portfolio. Diversify it.* Don't concentrate risk, particularly if you have accumulated a good deal of capital over a period of time. Some things will work out; others won't. The diversified portfolio protects your wealth against the impact of loss in one or a few areas of investment. It minimizes the chance of overall loss.

20. *Think of your dollars as your inventory.* In the same way that groceries are the grocer's inventory, your dollars are your inventory, your working assets. Don't spend more money this year simply because you have some dollars that you did not have last year. Be happy that your capital has grown. Conserve it, and invest the capital gain so that your additional cash won't simply provide an opportunity to spend.

21. *Don't oversocialize.* Cocktail parties and golf games are short-term activities, finished as soon as you go home. Work and study are investments in the future. They have a "carry forward." Socializing can develop into an all-consuming activity, never leaving time for concentration on long-term projects, of which wealth-building is one. Also, oversocializing can be money-consuming as well as time-consuming.

22. *Avoid the feeling of greed in your capital-building activities.* Greed is the greatest enemy of capital-building. It is supposed to underlie the capitalist system, according to some political and economic writers. Actually, you should work "easily" in developing a business or in developing wealth. Don't try to wring every last nickel out of your capital-building activities. And don't try to grab too much too soon as this may result in your ending up with nothing. If you are inclined to "count your gold" periodically and then spend time speculating as to how you can make twice as much in half the time, remind yourself that greed can destroy your wealth-building program.

23. *Set up a system of priorities.* Decide what is most important and work on that first or longest or both. For example, don't take days to buy a set of tires at the lowest possible price. Shop for about an hour, buy the tires, and then concentrate on locating investments which, if well chosen, may very well earn enough in a few days to pay for several sets of tires.

If $10,000 comes back to you from an investment, sit down immediately and begin planning where to place the money again. Don't put it into the first opportunity that appears. Spend plenty of time planning where to place it, and spend the time right away. This is a first-priority activity of the wealth-builder.

Most people, investors included, do not establish priorities according to economic importance to guide them in their wealth-building activities. In fact, most investors fall down worst of all by failing to take their investment portfolios seriously enough to devote the time and energy required to invest for maximum growth in the future.

24. *Associate with achievers.* Regardless of the field in which they operate, associate with those who are active and achieving their goals. Try to spend some time with friends and acquaintances who are developing businesses and who are moving ahead in various fields. It is obviously most beneficial to you to associate with those who in one way or another are building wealth. The mental attitude of these achievers is likely to influence you in a positive way. If you associate with lazy people or plodders, you will tend to remain on their level or to be pulled down to their level. Your friends and associates tend to pull you up or pull you down—or let you remain where you are right now.

This writer's association with J. Paul Getty was an example of being "pulled up." After being hired away from the government by Getty, he said to himself, "Let's see just what Paul Getty has done in order to become wealthy. Maybe I can learn something. Maybe, in fact, I can become wealthy too, not as wealthy as Getty, of course, but at least to a degree wealthy."

25. *Think positively.* If you can't think positively right now, then *try* to think positively. By constantly trying, you may be able to develop a positive outlook. Without a positive outlook, it is difficult to build wealth—or anything else.

Think positively and optimistically about what you are doing today, about your future, and about your wealth-building program. Overcome negativism as much as you can. Discipline yourself. Become knowledgeable in your field, because with knowledge of your subject comes confidence, which is necessary for a positive approach.

If you are sincere in trying to develop a positive and constructive outlook, doors may well open to you and you may receive help in building wealth.

In 1975 we asked J. Paul Getty whether anything ever

"got him down" since we were always impressed with his positive outlook. He replied simply, "No, nothing ever does get me down." This was his attitude despite the fact that, along with his good fortune financially, Paul Getty had enough misfortune to discourage anyone who did not possess tremendous inner strength.

Some people seem to have been born with an optimistic outlook. Others have learned to be optimistic. And there are some people who appear to have been negative since birth but eventually may learn to be optimistic. However one starts out and despite difficulties which may seem insurmountable, one should at least try to see the brighter side of life. Armed with knowledge and thinking confidently and positively, one holds the key to success in any endeavor, including wealth-building.

Index